You can never take what you love too seriously...

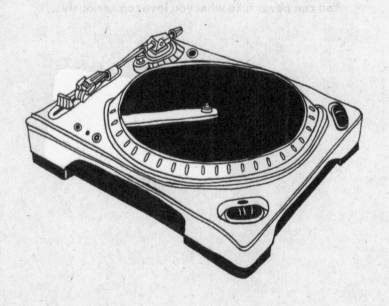

The Periodic Table Series

Periodically, we're all geeks about the things we love and the Periodic Table Series has been created to celebrate this universal fact.

Inspired by The Periodic Table of Chemical Elements*, our experts have applied scientific logic to an eclectic range of subjects that regularly baffle beginners and fire-up fans. The outcome of this experiment is the essential guide you hold in your hand.

Geeky? Absolutely.
Hugely satisfying? Categorically.

*The Periodic Table of Chemical Elements orders all the known matter that makes up our world, from hydrogen to helium, by chemical properties and behaviour to give scientists a handy overview of a rather complex subject.

THE PERIODIC TABLE OF
HIP HOP

NEIL KULKARNI

EBURY
PRESS

2

Ebury Press, an imprint of Ebury Publishing,
20 Vauxhall Bridge Road,
London, SW1V 2SA

Ebury Press is part of the Penguin Random House
group of companies whose addresses can be found
at global.penguinrandomhouse.com

Penguin
Random House
UK

Copyright © Ebury Press 2015
Illustrations © Hennie Haworth 2015

First published by Ebury Press in 2015
This paperback edition published by Ebury Press
in 2024

www.eburypublishing.co.uk

A CIP catalogue record for this book is available
from the British Library

ISBN: 9781529937688

Printed and bound in Great Britain by Clays Ltd,
Elcograf S.p.A.

The authorised representative in the EEA is
Penguin Random House Ireland, Morrison
Chambers, 32 Nassau Street, Dublin D02 YH68

Penguin Random House is committed to a
sustainable future for our business, our readers
and our planet. This book is made from Forest
Stewardship Council® certified paper.

Contents

The Periodic Table of
HIP HOP

PRE-HIP HOP | OLD SCHOOL | NEW SCHOOL

MAINSTREAM

1 **Jb** 56 James Brown		10 **Kb** 79 Kurtis Blow	14 **W** 83 Whodini				
2 **Gc** 59 George Clinton	5 **Kh** 74 Kool Herc	11 **Gt** 80 Grand Wizard Theodore	15 **Rd** 84 Run-DMC	22 **Bb** 86 Beastie Boys	28 **Bd** 88 Big Daddy Kane	33 **Kr** 87 KRS-One	39 **It** 86 Ice-T
3 **Wp** 69 Watts Prophets	6 **Gf** 79 Grandmaster Flash	12 **Tt** 79 Treacherous Three	16 **Sp** 86 Salt n Pepa	23 **Ll** 85 LL Cool J	29 **Er** 86 Eric B and Rakim	34 **Um** 88 Ultramagnetic MCS	40 **Nw** 88 N.W.A.

UNDERGROUND

| 4 **Is** 67 Iceberg Slim | 7 **Ab** 80 Afrika Bambaataa | 13 **Cc** 82 Cold Crush Brothers | 17 **Sc** 85 Schoolly D | 24 **Pe** 87 Public Enemy | 30 **Sl** 88 Slick Rick | 35 **Du** 89 Digital Underground | 41 **Ee** 88 Eazy-E |
| | 8 **Mm** 79 Melle Mel | | 18 **Ff** 82 Fab 5 Freddy | 25 **Ep** 88 EPMD | 31 **Bz** 88 Biz Markie | 36 **Ji** 86 Just-Ice | 42 **Gb** 89 Geto Boys |

PRODUCERS & LABELS

| | 9 **Sr** 52 Sylvie Robinson | | 19 **Ku** 85 Kurtis Mantronik | 26 **Rs** 80 Russell Simmons | 32 **Ma** 87 Marley Marl | 37 **Rp** 81 Robbins and Plotnicki | 43 **Jh** 86 Jerry Heller |
| | | | | 27 **Rr** 84 Rick Rubin | | 38 **Lp** 90 Large Professor | 44 **Dd** 86 Dr Dre |

EQUIPMENT

20 **Rt** 80 Roland TR-808	21 **Eu** 87 E-mu SP-1200

ELEMENT KEY
TOP LEFT: ELEMENT NUMBER
TOP RIGHT: YEAR OF FIRST RELEASE

45 89 **De** De La Soul			62 94 **Na** Nas	68 91 **Ch** Cypress Hill				90 04 **Kw** Kanye West
46 89 **Tq** A Tribe Called Quest	51 91 **Gs** Gang Starr	56 91 **Tu** Tupac	63 94 **Bs** Biggie Smalls	69 94 **Di** D.I.T.C.	74 93 **Wu** Wu-Tang Clan	79 94 **O** Outkast	84 96 **Jz** Jay-Z	91 07 **Nm** Nicki Minaj
47 88 **Ju** Jungle Brothers	52 92 **P** Pharcyde	57 93 **Sd** Snoop Dogg	64 93 **Md** Mobb Deep	70 93 **Ak** Alkaholiks	75 95 **Ra** Raekwon	80 97 **Lj** Lil Jon	85 99 **Em** Eminem	92 10 **Kl** Kendrick Lamar
48 91 **Bl** Black Sheep	53 91 **Ms** Main Source	58 90 **Ic** Ice Cube	65 93 **Bm** Black Moon	71 92 **R** Redman	76 95 **Gz** GZA	81 95 **Mp** Master P	86 97 **Me** Missy Elliott	93 08 **Of** Odd Future
49 86 **Kd** Kool DJ Red Alert	54 91 **Km** KMD	59 95 **Wc** WC and the Maad Circle	66 97 **Se** Sean Combs	72 92 **St** Steve Rifkind	77 96 **Rl** Real Live	82 94 **Ds** DJ Screw	87 95 **Ro** Roots	94 11 **Ck** Chief Keef
50 89 **Pp** Prince Paul	55 89 **Dp** DJ Premier	60 91 **Sk** Suge Knight	67 92 **Pr** Pete Rock	73 93 **B** Beatnuts	78 93 **Rz** RZA	83 97 **Jd** J Dilla	88 95 **N** Neptunes	
	61 94 **Wg** Warren G						89 97 **T** Timbaland	

Introduction

This is the story of, perhaps, the only genuinely new artistic innovation of the twentieth century after jazz. Hip hop is a culture, a dissident art movement, a way of thinking and being. Hip hop is not something you do, it is something you are, and essentially a culture of resistance.

What hip hop teaches you is that you don't have to wait for freedom, you can claim it through art. You can say *anything*. You can sound like *anything*. You can use *anything*. Once hip hop has put that lesson inside your young mind it utterly transforms the way you see and interpret the world. Everything becomes usable, stealable and malleable. Anything lyrical, musical, poetic, intellectual, political, emotional, can be reconfigured by hip hop in the act of pursuing your imagination. Hip hop teaches you to refuse conventional ways of doing things and find your own way of putting the world together, or breaking it apart. Thus, this book resists official history.

Official history dictates that hip hop is made of four elements: b-boying (incorrectly labelled breakdancing), graffiti, rapping and DJing. Heads up straight off: there's little about breaking and graffiti in this book. I see both as far more linked with older adversarial and competitive forms of interaction than being essential to hip hop's birth. What they've both bequeathed to hip hop is a spirit of competitiveness. The battle is a vital element of hip hop. No matter what aspect you specialise in, if you're an untested talent, and unwilling to stand your skills up next to others, to test your abilities in live competition or performance, you will be regarded with suspicion and doubt. Hence the still livid detestation of 'Internet rappers' among many hip-hop fans and artists: the innate mistrust of any performer who can't cut it in a real face-to-face sense, live.

For me, that competitive edge in hip hop comes from much older motifs in black American culture. It does not start with some Bronx origin myth. In the beginning there was the word. It was held in the head, nurtured in the heart and exploded in the mouth of the Griots, West African travelling troubadours. The word attached to a beat, a tune, played on gut and skin and wood. Words about anything the singer damn well wanted to be about, but these poets were hired guns, hired for their knowledge, their possibilities of lyrical devastation. They were spokesmen and -women for a people. Local, humorous, insulting, improvised, political, sexual, celebratory, gossipy, satirical, changing depending on geography and commission, the work of the Griots set the template for so much of what would be called pop music.

After these same West African troubadours were taken from their nations with whips and chains and transplanted halfway across the globe, the blues, jazz, soul, funk and eventually rap music emerged from that buried, unforgotten tradition. A connection negated by hip hop's tendencies towards social conscience (Griots never had such lofty ambitions – the point was to offer poetical succour to the powerful and get paid) but a connection that looks more and more real the further that hip hop turns into pure commerce. Although the connection between Griots and rap music has been overstated in the past there's no denying that if hip hop is an American culture, like all non-native American cultures it emerged from a process of bastardisation, theft and tradition that undoubtedly includes the Griots, and is now encoded deep in its DNA.

Fast forward to 1939 and a Yale psychologist named John Dollard travels to the Jim Crow South to study the personality development of black children. He finds a game that nags at him: kids and adults, in towns and cities and villages, on street corners and schoolyards, facing off verbally, insulting each other profanely, creatively. Dollard recognised a tradition that traced back to the Griots and led forward to black comedy and hip hop: the Dozens.

Dollard reported, 'The jests fly – about infidelity, though each seems a faithful husband – about impotence, though both are apparently adequately married and have children – about homosexual tendencies, although neither exhibits such to public perception.'

Improvisatory, competitive, the Dozens bled into jazz, barrel-house bawdiness and, of course, rap. Authors in the Harlem renaissance like Langston Hughes and Ralph Ellison tapped into the direct playfulness and artistry of the Dozens. Black comedians like Richard Pryor paid homage. Crucially, the social purpose of the Dozens is something rap has inherited. In a world in which black American males are routinely talked about inhumanely, denigrated and dehumanised, this game teaches you not only how to deal with insults but also dole them out, amplified. It showed how to use your mouth to cope with day-to-day oppression, releasing the tension. Battle-rhyming in rap relies crucially on the abilities that the Dozens rely upon – coming up with something so creatively obscene and shocking that your opponent is stunned into mute acquiescence. This is poetry as game, as pleasure, as play, as survival tactic. Braggadocio rap in a nutshell.

Similarly competitive, breaking or b-boying was a style of dance that grew in the early seventies funk clubs, busted out on to the streets, and became most closely connected to the growing avant-garde art of hip hop. It was predicated on your ability to test your steps against others, in non-violent no-contact confrontations called uprock battles. These battles were where your skills in the basic steps of b-boying (the top-rock and the six-step) could be elaborated out into a dizzying myriad of moves: the Worm, the Jackhammer, the Head-spin, the Flare, the Floor-lock, the Hand-glide. End on the Freeze. Breaking, like all hip hop, has polyglot and apocryphal influences and it could've grown from the Good Foot and James Brown, from Sophie Tucker's Worm-moves of the 1920s, equally from the Run Run Shaw kung-fu movies playing in the grindhouses of NYC on a constant basis, or perhaps from Latino/Brazilian capoeira martial arts. In the clubs, blocks, church halls, youth centres and community arenas of 1970s New York, b-boying was its own community and hip-hop music was its soundtrack. As one of the 'four pillars' of hip hop it would go through the quickest cycle of media misreading and misportrayal with the commercial exploitation that inevitably followed. A lot of breakers are featured in these pages but only when they made the move from the dance floor to the microphone or the turntable. Hip hop may well have entertained the same kids, but to understand hip hop I don't think you need to be a dancer or a spray-can artist. You need to listen. I've focused on the music and have broken my periodic table up accordingly.

A brief note also here about 'hip-hop fashion'. There's none in this book because there's no such thing. Hip hop follows the street. This isn't a book about street fashion or changing trends in sportswear, high-street couture, or how to cut yourself a nice hi-top fade. It's a book about hip-hop culture and, for me as a fan, absolutely pre-eminent in that is the music. Thus, the vast bulk of this book is about rappers and DJs. I've also included columns that reflect the impact labels, technology and individual producers have had on hip-hop music. Even with that limitation there are inevitable oversights. The most important rapper in the world can't be mentioned here because that's the rapper you haven't heard yet, the one who's going to drop that track next week that'll totally blow your mind. Hip hop constantly moves forward so any attempt to provide a definitive overview of its history is inevitably flawed in that it's going to miss that next fix, that next rapper, that next producer who finds a way to send hip hop in another direction. Another thing I've probably had to leave out is *your* favourite rapper. Hey, I know how it hurts, I've left out plenty of *my* favourite rappers. It's simply not possible to fit in everyone I wanted to when telling a broad story about hip hop.

How the table works

I have kept my table strictly US-based. It's a story that comes together on the East Coast, swings out to the West Coast during the 'Golden Age' (more on that ambivalent term anon) and finally spreads all over the continent. Because I've focused on US hip hop from its birth to its current diaspora (and much-mooted 'death') I've left out global scenes in hip hop like French rap, UK rap, African rap. All of these, with their different roots, sub-genres, histories and offshoots, deserve their own books. I've also only been able to mention tangentially all the ways in which hip hop has influenced and affected other musical cultures, from rock and metal through to brilliant bastardisations like drum and bass, jungle, electro and grime. Each of those errant stepchildren deserves its own book also. In the introductions to each era, and also the entries for each figure, I've attempted to pull in all those extra-musical and non-musical factors that have had a massive influence on hip hop.

The table progresses left to right along loosely chronological lines. Starting with those few avatars who predicted and pre-dated rap, the table then progresses through the 'Old School' period of 1974 to 1983, a period where it could be argued that hip hop hadn't even got a name yet.

The 'New School' period, which takes in 1983 to 1987, was the years in which hip hop was at the brink of being absorbed into pop but recalibrated itself and strongly asserted itself as its own genre. Hardcore rap emerged during this time and changed its sound and style.

The 'Golden Age' is a loaded term, but I'm using it here to mean a purely temporal period. I feel it can safely be defined as the decade from 1988 to 1998 when hip hop was creatively at a peak of imagination, diversity and artistry, both from rappers and producers. The danger is when the Golden Age becomes something to be yearned for again, a set of rules to attempt to replicate; some terrible rap music was made in the Golden Age and I've reflected that as well.

I hope you don't get the sense from the final part of the table, the 'Diaspora', that there isn't great hip hop being made right now. It's crucial that hip hop broke away from the East Coast/New York vs West Coast/LA straight-jacket it had been trapped in and started exploding out of the provincial and regional areas that had until then been silent. There is, every week, something new and mind-blowing to hear in rap. It's only in this millennium that I feel hip hop and rap music started becoming truly synonymous in public consciousness, and within hip hop culture itself. The pursuit of hip-hop culture has become all about music, all about rapping. I would only argue that finding rap that's genuinely new, despite the glut on offer in the Internet-age, is getting harder and harder thanks to the infiltration of rap by commerce and big business. I get angry in the 'Diaspora' section for which I make no apologies. I fiercely refute, however, arguments that rap music is dead. As long as MCs keep spitting and DJs keep flexing, rap music has life.

Though nearly everyone involved in hip hop fancies themselves as able to create a hip-hop track, the 'Producers' row collates those sonic technicians who've really made a difference in the sound of hip hop. As rare figures, inevitably they feature in a 'rare-metals' style adjunct of the main table.

Another note about structure: the higher up the table the element is, the more likely it is to be a mainstream name, known by non-fans as much as hip-hop fans themselves. This is where you'll find the big familiar stars, the names that mainstream pop audiences have been most directed towards. Consequently it's also where you might find the most 'controversial' opinions. The lower down the table you go the more likely it is you'll find underground, less-known names, those secret gems in hip hop who are in danger of being forgotten. Each column contains artists who share influences, a style, a sound, a producer or even a subject matter. If you like the more popular names at the top of a column you should investigate the more unheralded names beneath it. This is not a 'buyer's guide', but the discography at the end of the book should help further reconnaissance. In fact, as hip hop is such a fast-moving, multi-faceted culture it's inevitable that so many names have been left out but some of them are included in the discography.

Any book about hip hop can only fit in what the writer thinks is important. This book is a launch pad, not a dead end, and in it I hope I've managed to impart what's crucial about hip hop. That it is a revolutionary way of thinking and being that changes your life and saves lives on a daily basis. I owe it my past, present and future and I know I'm not alone. Dive in, go wander, find wonder. Hip hop, by definition, can never be what you think it is.

Pre-Hip Hop

Though hip hop's roots and tendrils, as mentioned in the introduction, can reach back into ancient history, I would argue that the formation of the hip-hop mindset – that strange, unique yet fertile combination of political, technological and cultural factors which created a world that needed hip hop, a world in which hip hop could form itself – only started coming together in the late 1960s.

A time of massive change in black America, a casting off of former confined roles, a lessening of some fears, an increase in some others, an outbreak of revolutionary sentiment and thought. And during this time of upheaval and change, black music underwent perhaps its greatest creative flowering since the birth of jazz.

The artists featured in this column comprise all the possibilities of ambition, artistry, focus and excess that would later map out the reaches of hip hop. In a crucial sense, hip hop's birth is a magical event, way more than merely the sum of its influences. But without the people featured here hip hop simply wouldn't sound or feel the way it does today. These aren't just elements, they're elemental spirits whose voices and sounds inhabit the very bloodstream of hip-hop culture. Every rap artist in this book, whether conscious, criminal, collective or solitary, can be traced back to one of these pre-hip hop avatars.

Column 1

1 56 **Jb** James Brown	
2 59 **Gc** George Clinton	**5** 74 **Kh** Kool Herc
3 69 **Wp** Watts Prophets	**6** 79 **Gf** Grandmaster Flash
4 67 **Is** Iceberg Slim	**7** 80 **Ab** Afrika Bambaataa
	8 79 **Mm** Melle Mel
	9 52 **Sr** Sylvie Robinson

JAMES BROWN

Brown's music – ancient, futurist, sophisticated, feral – is the foundation stone of so much hip hop simply in terms of borrowed grooves, stolen samples, twisted shards of horn and voice that end up being totemic hooks in so much rap music. Brown is perhaps only rivalled by Nola's The Meters in terms of familiarity and usage. Listen to his band. The horns of Fred Wesley and Hank Ballard, the scratchy guitar of Jimmy Nolen, the bass of Bootsy Collins and Sweet Charles Sherrell, the beats of Clyde Stubblefield and John 'Jabo' Starks – these are primal and recognisable elements of the hip-hop sound. Listening to any James Brown from that era sparks off a million memories of later rap tracks in the mind of any b-boy. As perhaps the most pivotal musical influence behind other crucial outfits like Sly and the Family Stone, Gil Scott-Heron and Funkadelic, his influence over hip hop's musical backdrop cannot be overestimated. His moves, his shake and surge, had a huge influence on the new steps and old shimmies inherent in early breaking. When, in 1969, he got on the Good Foot, replacing the Hustle with his own high-energy take, he laid down the dance steps that would be developed into the b-boy style.

Beyond that, though, James Brown's persona fed itself massively into hip hop's bloodstream. He exerted a fanatical, fractious control over his band, determined to build his community up. He said it loud about being black and proud while behind the scenes treating his musicians as something between slave and robot. James Brown was determined to outdo Motown's piffling dreams of self-sufficiency. His dream of dictatorially controlling a new and ruthless form of non-criminal black capitalism has rubbed off on every label boss and rap mogul since. A fulcrum of all the possibilities, ambitions, bad habits and broken dreams of black music in the twentieth century and beyond, it's simply not possible to listen to hip hop without hearing James Brown seeping through every note.

2	59
Gc	
George Clinton	

GEORGE CLINTON

If James Brown presaged the business-minded, aspirational, money-hungry capitalist side of what would become hip-hop culture then George Clinton and his P-funk collective foreshadowed hip hop's excessive side, its groggy psychedelic reach and range. Along with the musical possibilities that emerging hip-hop technology afforded producers in terms of keeping it unreal, P-funk emphasised the lyrical possibilities. Stevie Wonder had brought electronica into funk and P-funk took that to its ultimate exposition.

It's testament to the wide-open flexibility of Clinton and Co's ideas that they found themselves recycled by both the overtly conscious Native Tongues posse of rap crews *and* adopted as the primary sound-source for Dre's new imagining of West Coast gangsta-rap. P-funk music found its way into the sample-bank of hip hop from the off and has stayed there ever since.

Clinton proved that you didn't need to play an instrument or be able to sing to make incredible music. In contrast to James Brown's insistence on near-anonymity for his backing band, each of the players in P-funk had a unique character and persona, a chance to be as freaky as they wanted to be within the loose confines of the P-funk family. This chance to belong to a crew based on merit and personality and weirdness can be seen in every crew from N.W.A. and Public Enemy through to New-School outfits like Digital Underground and Wu-Tang Clan. Whenever hip hop has sought freaky strength in numbers, it's P-funk they're tipping a (frequently ridiculous) hat to. Everything from 'Maggot Brain' through to 'Atomic Dog' should be considered seminal texts.

3	69
Wp	
Watts Prophets	

WATTS PROPHETS

The Watts Prophets are here to represent the revolutionary collective. 'Rap' was something people did long before someone erected a mic between two turntables. Isaac

Hayes, James Brown, Gil Scott-Heron, Last Poets – they all talked about 'rapping', talking in a way that was subversive, real, in a code impenetrable to authority yet easily understandable to your confederates on the street. I doubt anyone who called themselves a rapper after hip hop first emerged had even heard the music of the Watts Prophets. But so prophetic were they, listening to them now it's as if their art was sent backwards from hip hop, retroactively born from the later supernova.

Free-jazz applied to poetry. A pipe-bomb of words thrust through your letterbox, drop-kicked at your head, hard. Hip hop before it knew its own name. The Last Poets will be the hip hop avatars you've heard of, the ones actually heard by white folk in the late sixties, the ones still recalled by official history as the first rap crew. The Watts Prophets remain an altogether more underground voice, but one undimmed by the passing of time and their relative enduring obscurity. Elegiac, furious, dazzling, the now near-forgotten *Black Voices On The Streets Of Watts* (1969) and *Rappin' Black In A White World* (1971) directly link Black Panther politics, nascent agit-funk doom, free-jazz glossolalia and an almost dub-sense of dread with words that could be sliced and diced over any new break or beat and would still sound like they were writ tomorrow. Yeah, Isaac Hayes rapped. Yeah, the Last Poets rapped. But no one rapped quite so ahead of the curve as the Watts Prophets. A decade ahead of their time.

4   67
Is
Iceberg Slim

ICEBERG SLIM

If the Prophets prefigured rap's conscious, socially revolutionary edge, then Slim mapped out a different illegality. His stories of the underworld criminal life touched with a perverse yet unmistakable moral sense, were, unlike many of the gangstas to come, genuinely informed by experience.

Born in 1918 in Chicago, Robert Lee Maupin was brought up in a middle-class household, a college boy

and contemporary of Ralph Ellison, author of the classic
novel *Invisible Man*. Maupin was an educated boy who
looked with envy when the local pimps brought their
charges into his mum's beauty salon. By 18 he was a pimp
himself, something he continued to be with coolness
(which together with his six foot two, ten-stone frame
gave him his nom de plume) and ruthlessness until the
age of 42. After a spell in jail, Slim, who considered
himself too old to continue in the pimp game, relocated
to LA, changed his name to Robert Beck, married, and
became a door-to-door insecticide salesman. His wife
encouraged him to write his life story and in 1967 his
autobiography *Pimp* was published. Changing names
to protect the guilty, absolutely refusing to glamorise
any aspect of his previous life, *Pimp* was a revelation to
everyone who read it. Although filed alongside similar
crime-memoirs by Eldridge Cleaver and Malcolm X, Slim's
writing occupied an altogether bleaker, more baleful,
place. In 1976, the album *Reflections* emerged, in which
Slim recited passages from *Pimp* over funky, understated
backing tracks by the Red Holloway Quartet. Listening
now, not only is Slim's voice imperial, masterly and utterly
compelling but the stories, the honesty of the stories,
the way his persona occasionally cracks into fear and
regret – all of it is laying down trails and transgressions
that later gangsta-rap would act as if it invented. Ice-T,
Ice Cube and Jay-Z would all pay homage. With his book
Pimp, Slim – now an almost forgotten figure – predicted
blaxploitation and whole swathes of black culture in the
seventies. Seek out *Reflections* and cool out to the OG.

Old School

For the first five years of its life, from 1974 to 1979, hip hop had no name; it was a culture that refused to be skewered by any firm nomenclature.

A curious yet notable comparison is with what was happening in Jamaican music at the time. Like jazz before it, reggae was music born in a brothel, and needed to last beyond the usual temporal limitations of performance. Like hip hop after it, reggae was a music that needed to get your attention via the loudest sound-system or most convincing MC. Like the other studio and club-based music it influenced later, reggae relied upon a secrecy and fierce competition between rivals. To protect their identities, DJs scratched off the inner circles on discs to create the first white labels, those sought-after totems of the DJ's art (Afrika Bambaataa would use water and then peel them off), MCs squashed rivals with light-speed verbals dripping with Dozens-style disdain. Listen to U-Roy's toasting on King Tubby records and the spontaneity, the live chatty jive-talking, seems almost a direct precursor of rap. The success of artists like U-Roy and Dillinger undoubtedly made the world readier to accept the MC as artist in their own right.

Likewise, behind the decks or desk, reggae's focus on weed-infused post-production finds uncanny echo in eighties and nineties hip hop. The producer/DJ as sorcerer, the backing track as a mere starting point for the creation of music that can't actually be played by human beings – these are ideas that hip-hop producers would make their own. While the connection between rap and reggae is often overstated, perhaps down to how many of hip hop's first wave had family roots back in Jamaica, it's too simplistic to simply graft analogous practice here and to trace rapping back to toasting, scratching back to dubbing. Yet without reggae and dub, hip hop simply wouldn't be the way it is. Simultaneously, in Kingston and the Bronx, new roles in music were being configured. Not by bands, but by DJs and hype-men.

Column 2

1 **56** **Jb** James Brown		**10** **79** **Kb** Kurtis Blow
2 **59** **Gc** George Clinton	**5** **74** **Kh** Kool Herc	**11** **80** **Gt** Grand Wizard Theodore
3 **69** **Wp** Watts Prophets	**6** **79** **Gf** Grandmaster Flash	**12** **79** **Tt** Treacherous Three
4 **67** **Is** Iceberg Slim	**7** **80** **Ab** Afrika Bambaataa	**13** **82** **Cc** Cold Crush Brothers
	8 **79** **Mm** Melle Mel	
	9 **52** **Sr** Sylvie Robinson	

KOOL HERC

You could say that before Herc, and outside of the Bronx, the DJ as king was already going strong in NYC. DJ Hollywood and his MC Eddie Cheeba were rocking downtown clubs with a mix of funk and hype-chat well before Herc threw his first party. But Herc was the guy who stumbled upon hip hop's truly revolutionary heart and brought it not just to those who could afford to get into clubs, but to kids and adults in parks and rec rooms and basketball courts. If you were in the dilapidated South Bronx in the early seventies, one of the few non self-destructive things you could do was go to one of Kool Herc's parties in a rec room at 1520 Sedgwick Ave. By 1973, the Jamaican-born Herc was a legend in the Bronx but he was always looking for ways to make his parties better than anyone else's.

He noticed that the crowd loved it when the drum beats took over in the funk and soul records he was playing. He realised that by using two copies of the same record he could loop the instrumental breaks into infinite space. He experimented in his apartment, mixing one break into the break of another song. He called that doing a 'merry-go-round' and it became part of his arsenal of DJing tricks. He became a folk hero in the Bronx, his parties rammed. With his sets now resembling something approaching reappropriated art, Herc realised that he was too busy on the decks to MC so enlisted his friend Coke La Rock to take over MCing duties. Perhaps this was the first time in history that two turntables and a microphone had been used for something beyond the music being played, to create a vibe that's uniquely its own. La Rock's rhymes weren't written, were purely improvised, more akin to Jamaican toasting, phrases like 'Hotel, no tell' and 'Ya rock and ya don't stop' crept into the lexicography. Herc's parties started commanding huge crowds around the Bronx. A core of talent watched, learned and built on Herc's foundation, namely Grandmaster Flash, Grandwizard Theodore and Afrika

Bambaataa. Despite Herc's own tendency to overstate his 'creation' of hip hop, without a doubt he's the font from which most of what would be called hip hop would flow for the rest of the seventies. His disciples would make sure of that.

GRANDMASTER FLASH

Flash is fast. Flash is cool. If Herc was the discoverer of hip hop's revolutionary musical mindset then Flash finessed that discovery, perfected it, pursued it technologically and imaginatively, and exploded the template to a sense of cohesion and possibility. Like Herc, Flash could trace his roots back to the Caribbean. Like Afrika Bambaataa, he had the benefit of growing up with a parent who had a large record collection: Flash's dad had an extensive set of rare soul and Jamaican music. This, coupled with his education in electronics (insisted upon by his vocationally minded mum), meant that when Flash watched Herc perform, he went home not just fired up by Herc's ideas but also keen to use his expertise and musical knowledge to force the form to new heights. He was playful with his experimentation but also obsessive, spending days in his room perfecting techniques he'd then try out at parties, techniques that are now staples of any hip-hop DJ's arsenal. Flash took Herc's merry-go-round and turned it into quick-mix backspins, looping beats infinitely with lightning-speed seamlessness. His punch phrasing elaborated on those looped beats, dropping in horn and string stabs to dramatise and punctuate the endless grooves. He took Grandmaster Wiz's scratching technique and turned it into something precise and devastating, a signature sound that is still immediately identifiable and uniquely belongs to hip hop.

Flash's virtuosity on the wheels of steel was without peer, and with Herc's career effectively ended after a nightclub stabbing it was Flash that stepped in to become the hottest DJ in the Bronx. It's arguable, because we weren't there, how much of Flash's artistry was noticed in the clubs; frequently, as any DJ knows, it was volume rather than finesse that really worked a crowd and built a reputation. But without Flash's innovations in cutting, mixing and scratching, hip hop wouldn't sound anything like it does now and it would, perhaps, never have progressed musically beyond the parties it started in. Hip hop was becoming innovative sound-manipulative art. The step downtown and outwards to the world was on.

AFRIKA BAMBAATAA

Bambaataa was the Old-School figure who held out longest against recording, the Amon Ra of hip-hop culture. He was raised in the Bronx as Keith Donovan by a mother whose radical politics, and extensive and enormous record collection, would influence her son's later musical development. After being transformed by a trip to Africa in the mid-seventies that utterly upended his world-view, Donovan returned to the Bronx, renaming himself Afrika Bambaataa Aasim after an early twentieth-century Zulu rebel chief. He soon set about doing everything he could to excel in the burgeoning hip-hop culture as a DJ while keeping an eye on how this nascent culture could be appropriated towards more positive and revolutionary aims.

As a DJ, Bambaataa picked up a rep for being an adventurous 'master of records', selecting the weirdest, most obscure cuts, interpolating pop-cultural detritus like the 'Pink Panther Theme' into his mixes and armed with the loudest and most fearsome sound-system in the five boros. By 1976, inspired by Herc and equipped by Disco King Mario, Bambaataa started organising block parties and battles all over the South Bronx. By 1977, alongside his DJ crew the Organization, he created the Universal Zulu Nation, a confederacy of rappers, graffiti artists, breakers and DJs (including Jazzy Jay, who would later go on to record 'It's Yours' with T LA Rock and, in the process, create Def Jam Records) thoroughly committed to being a positive force within the black and Latino communities of NYC. He continued to DJ at increasingly bigger venues through 1978 to 1979, breaking out of the ghetto and bringing the Zulu Nation to Manhattan clubs via support slots with the likes of Bow Wow Wow. In 1981 he utterly transformed the future of music with 'Planet Rock', a single he created with Arthur Baker and John Robie. Melding the stiff funkativity of Kraftwerk's 'Trans-Europe Express' and 'Numbers' with the contrasting vibes of George Clinton, Gary Numan and Yellow Magic Orchestra, 'Planet Rock' became an international underground hit and in one fell swoop birthed electro-funk. 'Looking For The Perfect Beat' perfected the form and Bambaataa never made anything as important afterwards. As a nexus of all the different strands feeding into hip hop's birth and all the different strands that led away from that moment, Bambaataa is exemplary.

MELLE MEL

Just as Flash became the first DJ to expand his role beyond tune selection and the provision of massive volume, so Melle Mel can legitimately be seen as the first hip-hop MC to see his role as more than just chatting nonsense and hyping the crowd. Mel wrote so he could properly interrogate a subject through his raps, focus his rhymes at a certain specific target and maintain that locked-on feel that starts turning rap away from being pure technique and towards being its own new way of saying things, its own new way of *thinking* about things. The complexity of Flash's mixing meant his own mic-skills suffered as a result and consequently he needed a crew of MCs to flesh out his sound: Cowboy brought charisma and looseness; Kid Creole brought non-stop patter and rhymes; Creole's brother, Melle Mel, brought something altogether unique: a jazzy confidence on the mic that matched Flash's improvisational confidence on the wheels of steel. When Flash's three MCs expanded, with the addition of Rahiem and Scorpio (stolen after a smack-down battle with rival crew Brothers Disco and the Funky Four MCs) to become the Furious Five, it was still Mel's voice that stood out, a voice that carried an authority and commanding presence unlike anyone else in rap at the time. From early Furious Five singles on the label Enjoy, like 'Superappin' through to the monster-hit success of 'White Lines' and 'The Message', for a lot of the world Mel's was the first rap voice that really demanded our attention, that really introduced us to the power of rap music, its shifting priorities and ability to investigate and talk about things no other type of pop music seemed to talk about. Perhaps more than anyone else in the first wave of Old-School pioneers, because of those two singles Melle Mel was *the* sound of rap music for a worldwide generation. From then on, rap didn't have to fear seriousness, didn't have to think its form could not sustain heavy narratives, deep thought, and elegant rage.

SYLVIE ROBINSON

In 1978, hip hop had still not found mainstream success mainly because it wasn't concerned with finding mainstream success. If you wanted to hear rapping outside of the club/park/gym then you needed to get your hands on a mix-tape. Mr Magic aka Lucky the Magician aka John Rivas was a custom speaker-builder who worked in a Manhattan electronics store during the day, and at night was unleashed across the airwaves in early 1979 for a two-hour 2am–4am show on the Upper West Side station WHBI that featured breaks and some of the earliest rappers. The growing vogue for Herc/Flash-style DJing meant some small labels were taking notice, bringing out bootleg 'Super Disco Break' compilations precisely for the growing army of deck-wrecking kids who attempted to emulate their DJ heroes. They sold well, but no one was releasing rap records. Most people who ran labels considered the music no more than a fad, a gimmick. The big DJ names, Flash, Bambaataa, resisted the move to vinyl, aware of how the culture might be diluted in contact with the mainstream. At this point, most rappers saw rapping as something that lasted for hours, that was live and improvised and could never be chopped into the three-minute chunk that was pop music's customary format. Harlemite Sylvie Robinson, the woman behind Sugar Hill Records, bypassed the doubts and resistance of the Bronx hardcore crowd by hiring three rappers from New Jersey and furnishing them with rhymes stolen from a Grandmaster Caz tape. Along with session men, they recreated the huge groove behind Chic's 'Good Times' and rushed out 'Rapper's Delight' by the Sugarhill Gang, the first ever hip-hop single. Together with the Fatback Band's 'Personality Jock' it proved, with incessant airplay and sold-out status everywhere it was stocked, that the radio was ready for rap, some stations even playing the full 15-minute version. Sugar Hill Records weren't affiliated with the RIAA (the official industry body of the US record industry) so Robinson made fake gold discs and plaques for her artists and paid the Sugarhill Gang a pitiful cut of 'Rapper's Delight' royalties to keep them from asking questions.

Vinyl enabled the culture to spread and Sugar Hill Records were essential in bringing hip hop to a wider audience. For some, this marked the start of the story, for others this was more like the end of the beginning. The success of Sugar Hill's methods saw a roughneck culture, a culture untutored in conventional pop performance, suddenly get togged out in wild outfits, taught dance routines, given a polished sense of presentation. Hip hop's first wave of talent was stepping out and on to the roller coaster of world tours, promo and recording that comes with being a pop star. Sugar Hill's naivety, exploitativeness and hucksterism would keep on reappearing in the hip-hop business. From here on in, that's what an awful lot of hip hop is: a business.

Column 3

10 **79** **Kb** Kurtis Blow	**14** **83** **W** Whodini

5 **74** **Kh** Kool Herc	**11** **80** **Gt** Grand Wizard Theodore	**15** **84** **Rd** Run-DMC
6 **79** **Gf** Grandmaster Flash	**12** **79** **Tt** Treacherous Three	**16** **86** **Sp** Salt n Pepa
7 **80** **Ab** Afrika Bambaataa	**13** **82** **Cc** Cold Crush Brothers	**17** **85** **Sc** Schoolly D
8 **79** **Mm** Melle Mel		**18** **82** **Ff** Fab 5 Freddy
9 **52** **Sr** Sylvie Robinson		**19** **85** **Ku** Kurtis Mantronik

Like all the best myths, the impact upon hip hop of the New York City blackouts in 1977 is a tall tale you'd love to be true.

After lightning strikes that overpowered and shut down electricity processing plants, in the evening of 13 July 1977 the power went out in all five boros of NYC. It was the long hot summer of the Son of Sam killings, and a brutal heat wave that accompanied a long period of economic penury for NYC (in 1975 Gerald Ford had denied federal funds to the bankrupt city leading to the famous *Daily News* headline the next day 'Ford To City: Drop Dead'). In the Bronx, a neighbourhood already ravaged by years of unemployment and violence, block parties that were sapping power from the streetlights suddenly ground to a halt. Many businesses had already closed for the night, those that hadn't hurried to do so, but for many it was too late. The mass-looting and vandalism that accompanied the blackout were in sharp contrast to the altogether cheerier blackouts of 1965. Those blackouts ended up being immortalised in Doris Day movies; these blackouts ended up changing the course of hip hop. Mass evacuations of the subways were accompanied by looting across the Bronx and Brooklyn – particularly from audio-equipment stores. Kit that was only previously accessible to the likes of DJ Hollywood and Herc suddenly found itself liberated and put in the hands of anyone who happened to have the gall and the cheek to get themselves fitted out. DJ Wiz has stated that 'Before that blackout, you had maybe five legitimate crews of DJs. After the blackout you had a DJ on every block. It made a big spark in the hip-hop revolution.' An intriguing notion, that some of the earliest salvos in hip-hop history were created on stolen equipment; too neat, perhaps, that music that stole from other music would end up being pioneered on decks that themselves were acquired illegally. Without a doubt, though, the explosion in the sheer numbers of hip-hop crews after the blackout can't be simply put down to coincidence. Without it, who knows if hip hop would've survived beyond the careers of the few protagonists it had in 1975 and 1976?

KURTIS BLOW

Kb

Kurtis Blow

Harlem-born, Hollis Queens-living Kurtis Blow accomplished a lot of firsts in hip hop. He was the first MC from outside of the Bronx to get recognition, under the aegis of his manager Russell 'Rush' Simmons, who was the only man to promote rap shows in the New York boro of Queens. Simmons put Blow together with DJ Davy DMX, whose 12 crates of records (Flash had 17, Bam had 20) made him the biggest draw in Queens.

When Rocky Ford from *Billboard* magazine enquired as to who was responsible for papering most of Queens with flyers, the fly-poster DJ Run (later of Run-DMC) told him to hook up with Simmons, his elder brother. After attending a few parties with Simmons, Ford quit *Billboard* and set out to create a rap record with DJ Hollywood and Hollywood's hype-man Eddie Cheeba. Simmons pointed him instead towards Blow. As December 1979 approached, 'Christmas Rappin'' by Kurtis Blow was recorded with words by Ford and fellow *Billboard* dropout J.B. Moore and music by Simmons's long-time co-producer Larry Smith. Without a deal for it, Simmons dropped off test-pressings at record shops and told the storeowners that if they needed extra copies they should send requests to Polygram. These fake orders and requests hyped the record sufficiently to get Blow a deal with Mercury. This was the first time hip hop was touched by a major label, and only about the third time hip hop was released on record at all. First released in Europe, 'Christmas Rappin'' became a huge hit, backed with a Euro-wide tour (another first for hip hop), before it was imported back to the States. Now a bona-fide rap star, Blow recorded 'The Breaks' for

Mercury in spring 1980 and it became *the* dance hit of the year, the first real gold record in hip-hop history.

Blow was rap's first star, the template for every solo rap star that followed. His *Soul Train* appearance performing 'The Breaks' in 1980 is the moment that mainstream black America wakes up to hip hop in a big big way. For Simmons this is just the beginning.

GRAND WIZARD THEODORE

Most innovations in music rely on an ability to not read the manual, to disregard the official constraints of correct usage and to actually abuse the equipment you've got, to come at the technology with a neophyte innocence, a childlike curiosity, the desire to play with presets and limitations in an entirely juvenile sense and see what new noise can be created.

Grand Wiz was a Bronx-born protégé of Flash, but with his own unique contributions to give to hip-hop production and, like Flash and Herc, someone whose experimental abuse of equipment pointed the way towards whole new areas of soundscaping in hip hop.

Legend has it that Grand Wiz was playing records in his bedroom, loud. Fed up with the racket, his mum stomped in and ordered him to turn down the music. Looking away from the turntable to face her while she issued forth, like any naughty kid his hands couldn't help slowly moving the record back and forth. As his mother's hollering receded into the background, he realised that he was creating a whole new sound from the turntable and once she'd left the room he started playing with it. Months of experimentation followed before he dared introduce it at a party but, once he had, the sound of scratching was born.

In that moment, hip hop had found its own uniquely suitable sound, a *musique concréte* rupture in pop's normal flow, a sound that revealed the nuts and bolts of how the music was made, and a sound that hip hop could call entirely its own.

TREACHEROUS THREE

Spoonie Gee, Kool Moe Dee, LA Sunshine, DJ Easy Lee and Special K formed the Treacherous Three in the very early days of rap and spent a long time simply battling other crews. In 1979, after releasing his own solo record, Spoonie was guilt-ridden that he'd left his friends out of his debut and insisted that the next release by Enjoy Records (owned by his uncle Bobby Robinson) included a straight up T3 track. 'The New Rap Language' is a stone-cold classic, introducing New York to T3's uniquely fast, light-speed style, particularly the incredible rhyming of Spoonie and Kool Moe Dee.

To get a true flavour of just how revolutionary Treacherous Three were though, just how much snappier, tighter and faster they were than the veterans who'd been on the scene since the days of Herc, ignore the official releases and seek out the bootleg of Kool Moe Dee's confrontation with Busy Bee at the Harlem World club at the tail end of 1981. What you hear is not just an older MC being outpaced, you hear him being destroyed, torn apart syntactically, methodically, with dizzying rapidity and venom. Kool Moe Dee's speed of thought and speech is simply unlike anything else in rap at the time. Not only setting out the definitive rap battle tactics that would dictate battle-rap standards and proceedings ever since, Dee finessed a style of rap – fast, meaningful, heavy, needing of repeated rewinds to untangle every idea – that would go on to influence a whole generation of new rap talent from T LA Rock and LL Cool J through to the Ultramagnetic MCs and Rakim. Even today, you get the feeling that Kool Moe Dee could rip any new spitter apart in seconds. Making the mainstream rap manoeuvres of the Sugarhill Gang look awfully lumbering, Treacherous Three, perhaps more than any other Old-School rap crew, laid the template for what the eighties would bring to hip hop in terms of lyrical skill and creativity. Don't leave the twentieth century without hearing that bootleg.

13 82
Cc
Cold Crush
Brothers

COLD CRUSH BROTHERS

As the eighties dawned, with the Funky Four and Flash's Furious Five busy touring and making records (Flash finally appearing on something that bears his name with the stupendous 'The Adventures of Grandmaster Flash On The Wheels Of Steel') and a whole welter of artists releasing tracks independently, the Cold Crush Brothers were the crew that came to fill a gap in the South Bronx club scene. Grandmaster Caz's rhymes were sensational, live, spontaneous, vicious and utterly unlikely to be released or recorded by a label – the Cold Crush Brothers distributed tapes of their live performances that become endlessly passed around, copied and re-copied by neighbourhood kids into hip hop, including a young Run-DMC.

For many, the business side of hip hop was taking the fun out of the culture. Frequently unable to use existing music as the musical backdrop of releases, Sugar Hill artists were forced to use the uncanny mimicry of the Sugar Hill house band, Doug Wimbish, Skip McDonald and Keith LeBlanc. The official releases that hip-hop artists brought out were nowhere near as exciting as the bootlegs played by Mr Magic, the live tapes and stolen recordings that were passed by those in the know to friends and other b-boys and b-girls. For those kids, the sound of hip hop was not captured in studios or by labels but by the recordings created by crews like Cold Crush and their rivals such Fantastic Romantics from their live battles. For the first time in rap you could feel a massive gulf opening up between rap as presented to the wider culture (crossover/mainstream) and the sound as it existed in the clubs (the underground).

The Cold Crush Brothers oversaw that return from the brink of commercialism back to the hardcore basics of hip hop that would characterise the next half-decade of rap, forming a heavy influence on a whole new generation of rappers intent on keeping the art but never being diluted by the pressures of the industry. The wedge was in.

New School

The 'New School' phase of hip hop depends upon the death of the Old School. Hip hop's first piece of Old School myth-making comes in 1983 and effectively zips a body-bag over hip hop's first era.

Frequently unwatchable, maddeningly clichéd, yet, within the hip-hop community, *Wild Style* – the film directed by first-timer Charlie Ahearn – is the holy grail of rap cinema way more than mainstream cash-ins like the *Electric Boogaloo* movies or the lamentable *Beat Street*. The only thing remotely rivalling it is the even rarer *80 Blocks From Tiffany's*, Gary Weis's documentary of late seventies South Bronx gang life. In contrast to that film's hard-boiled gaze, *Wild Style*'s narrative is flimsy. Based on the exploits of real-life pioneering graffiti-artist Lee Quinones, it follows him, as Zorr, around New York's South Bronx in the early eighties, running the rail yards, sparring with rival graffiti gangs, hanging around hip-hop clubs, being feted by a Manhattan gallery, and finally returning to his roots by painting an entire downtown warehouse for New York's biggest ever hip-hop night. The live footage Ahearn captures features a stellar cast of early hip-hop culture: Fab 5, Busy Bee, Flash, Grand Wizard Theodore, the Fantastic Freaks, the Cold Crush Brothers, the Rocksteady Crew and Treacherous Three are all in on the action.

Wild Style is a neo-realist musical that takes five whole years of underground black culture and avant-garde art in New York and condenses it into an hour and a half. It was the one moment in hip hop's first ten years when the culture was afforded serious cinematic treatment. It was the clearest mark of the end of the Old School and the birth of the New. *Wild Style* looks back at the burgeoning hip-hop culture with wide innocent eyes. From here on in, hip hop's vision becomes steely, narrowed, focused. Its ambitions are no longer local or purely mercenary. They're enormous.

Column 4

10 **79** **Kb** Kurtis Blow	**14** **83** **W** Whodini
11 **80** **Gt** Grand Wizard Theodore	**15** **84** **Rd** Run-DMC	**20** **80** **Rt** Roland TR-808
12 **79** **Tt** Treacherous Three	**16** **86** **Sp** Salt n Pepa	**21** **87** **Eu** E-mu SP-1200
13 **82** **Cc** Cold Crush Brothers	**17** **85** **Sc** Schoolly D
	18 **82** **Ff** Fab 5 Freddy
	19 **85** **Ku** Kurtis Mantronik

14		83
	W	
	Whodini	

WHODINI

In 1982 black radio was entirely resistant to rap. Still seen predominantly as kids' music, advertisers balked at paying for ads on a rap show, convinced kids had no money to spend. The number one black radio station in New York was WBLS, which unexpectedly lured Mr Magic over from public radio to host shows every Friday and Saturday night. *Rap Attack*, as the shows were called, took off big-time, and became known to the NYC reps of British label, Jive Records. Jive wanted to put a hip-hop group together and asked Mr Magic for help. With most of the name-rappers bound by contracts, his studio assistant Jalil stepped up and together with his friend Ecstasy (and overseen by producer Thomas Dolby) they brought out 'Magic's Wand' which sold in sufficient numbers to keep Jive interested. Christened Whodini in homage to Magic, they recorded an eponymous debut for Jive that sat uneasily between electro-pop and funk but again sold enough to keep Jive on board. The new outfit also attracted the interest of Russell Simmons, keen to add to his growing stable of talent at Rush Management that already included Kurtis Blow, Larry Smith and Spyder D, whose demo 'Big Apple Rappin' proved to be a huge indie success in 1980. When scratch DJ Grandmaster Dee made himself known to Magic he was recruited in as Whodini's DJ and Simmons realises that tracks created by Larry Smith would be ideal for the Whodini sound. The second album *Escape* that came out in 1984 was unique, and became hip hop's first album to go platinum. For Simmons, it was proof that rather than trying to break into black entertainment's superstructure hip hop he'd do better collaborating with outsiders , those without an in-built snobbery towards rap. Whodini's rise proved that rap could sustain itself and battle with the biggest names in pop. What Simmons did next with Rick Rubin, which changed rap forever, wouldn't have happened without the enabling confidence that Whodini gave him. Out of the blue and still somewhat under the radar, Whodini was one of the most important groups in hip-hop history.

RUN-DMC

The New School can be characterised as that period when young fans of the music took it back, reclaimed it from artists who'd been suckered and entranced away by mere show business, and plunged it back into the Reagan-ravaged streets.

In late 1982 and early 1983, hip-hop records didn't sound like hip hop. They were essentially R'n'B records with rapping on them, created by bands, session players and producers. The crucially exciting thing about hip hop, the music made by scratch DJs, only figured as an effect, a detail, not the root of where the grooves and sounds came from.

This cleaning-up of rap extended to the way that rap crews were forced to look by companies like Sugar Hill Records. They were shoulder-padded, lavishly costumed and bare-chested, akin to the rock and glam and pop outfits their record companies felt they should be competing with. Run-DMC said 'fuck that' and wore black Wranglers, Kangols and lace-less sneakers like the kids they were and the felons they didn't want to end up as.

That simplification and redirection towards the street in their look was mirrored beautifully in their music. The lush disco, pop and electro textures that Bam and Flash and the Sugarhill Gang were mired in were body-slammed into pulverising drum-machine beats, brutally effective heavy bass and powerful rhyming that showed no interest at all in crossing over anywhere. The early singles and the first two albums, in bringing hip hop back to its roots and fans, created perhaps the first moment when that free-floating musical signifier of attitude, 'hardcore', could be applied to hip hop. Instantly, in the staccato harshness of the beats and the aggressive pride of the rhymes, Run-DMC made everything that had happened before sound old-fashioned, too slick and smarmy. Their onward moves, including incorporating heavy rock into their sound, circumvented MTV's racist 'urban' music policy and turned a whole generation of rock kids on to hip hop via 'Rock Box' and 'Walk This Way'. This makes them, perhaps, the most important rap crew of the New School. They were certainly the first to start tapping into that suburban white market that's still so important in sustaining hip hop (even as hip hop kills itself trying to deny it).

SALT N PEPA

Just as the Beastie Boys blazed a trail in terms of white people's acceptance of hip hop, and hip hop's acceptance of white people, so the three Queens from Queens, Salt n Pepa, were pioneers in increasing female presence in rap music, and opening a door whereby women could enjoy and create hip hop as equals to their male rivals.

Before Salt n Pepa's emergence in the mid-eighties, women were often seen as marginal and transient figures in rap, more often the target of male rappers' abuse or adoration than actual protagonists in the culture. In differing ways, Roxanne Shanté, Queen Latifah, Lauryn Hill, Nefertiti, Rah Digga, Missy Elliott, Nicki Minaj, Azealia Banks and every female rapper since owe a little to Salt n Pepa, who first kicked that door open with such unstoppable confidence and irresistible delight. 'Push It' was one of the biggest rap hits of the eighties and like so much of Salt n Pepa's best work it was both big big fun *and* a stridently honest statement of intent. They absolutely refuted the demure politeness expected of women in rap, and rejected the sexist submissive stereotypes of macho rap in favour of a flagrant, energetic, deeply honest interrogation of their own sexuality ('Let's Talk About Sex') and lives. Salt n Pepa were hip-hop feminists par excellence, carving out roles in rap that were unapologetically based on their own strength of character and interests. *Hot, Cool & Vicious,*

their greatest album, made them the first female act
in hip hop to get a gold or platinum record. From Salt
n Pepa onwards, women had a template they could
work with, fuck around with, and imprint with their own
personas. Absolute trailblazers.

SCHOOLLY D

17	85
Sc	
Schoolly D	

For Schoolly D and his DJ Code Money, hip hop, in its
desperation to be recorded and score hits, had become
inescapably estranged from its beginnings. A fatal split
had occurred between the DJ and the rapper, which
they intended to remedy with raw recording, nearly live,
with minimum rehearsal and minimum edits. Schoolly
produced, wrote, arranged and designed his first records
like the unforgettable 'I Hate Rock And Roll', 'Gucci Time',
'Gangster Boogie' and 'Saturday Night', and brought
out his self-titled debut album and the truly legendary
Saturday Night album entirely by himself with no
interference from anybody else. Silk-screening T-shirts,
block-printing flyers and album sleeves, selling mix-tapes,
rapping at block parties and basement parties, Schoolly D
was an inspirational model of DIY self-sufficiency.

Rap, in pulling from funk, had featured gang
characters before but really as details of bigger pictures
or local colour in wider tableaux. Schoolly D focused
on those characters, the hooligan kids who made up
much of hip hop's young black fan base. This wasn't
the braggadocio that would characterise so much
later gangsta-rap; rather Schoolly D was intrigued by
the mindset of the gang life, how it was enforced by
environment and could only be broken by revolution or
liberation. With bone-crunching beats and punchy, heavy
sampled textures coming from his spanking new SP-12,
the *Saturday Night* album is a woozy, brutal zenith for
eighties' hardcore hip hop.

Schoolly was always criticised for the deliberate
'simplicity' of his music and the depravity of his rhymes
– in fact, Philadelphia city officials advocated stores

removing it from their shelves after public complaints about the album's violent content and negative portrayal of West Philly – but those were precisely the things that made him, and still make *Saturday Night*, so compelling. Ice-T, the Geto Boys, N.W.A. – everyone who came since who called themselves gangsta should pay dues.

FAB 5 FREDDY

18   82
Ff
Fab 5
Freddy

When MTV finally saw hip hop as fit for exploitation and put together a pilot for the show *Yo! MTV Raps*, it was telling that two of the hosts were Run-DMC and Fab 5 Freddy. Fab 5 Freddy was a hugely visible figure in the culture that would become known as hip hop but he wasn't really a rapper and had never spun a record or his head. His family were heavily connected: his grandfather was buddies with Marcus Garvey, his godfather was Max Roach, his dad was in the Audubon Ballroom when Malcolm X was assassinated, Dizzy Gillespie and Miles Davis would drop in at the family home for dinner.

Fred wasn't a musician, he was a tagger, an artist, a painter, a catalyst, a blender of worlds. Spraying 'Bull 99' wherever he went, he'd skip school, visit museums and art galleries, where he noticed just how close to the work of Warhol and Lichtenstein the growing graffiti phenomenon that was infecting the walls, doors, trains and flyovers of his neighbourhood really was.

Initiated into Lee Quinones's illustrious graff-crew the Fabulous 5, Fred copped a new alias, Fab 5 Freddy. When Fred and Lee created their notorious 'Campbell Soup Train' it was shot by photo-documentarians of the South Bronx scene Henry Chalfant and Martha Cooper and was featured in *Village Voice*. Freddy found himself bringing Uptown graff and hip hop right to the heart of Manhattan's art and music scenes. In clubs and galleries, roller rinks and lofts, bands and breakers, DJs and filmmakers, MCs and painters, post-punk bands like Bow Wow Wow and high-artists like Jean-Michel Basquiat sized each other up, liked what they saw, and learnt from each other. Just as hip-hop music's essentially criminal mindset – steal and re-use what you can – is its unique response to its environment and times, so Freddy and Quinones's art is an essentially law-breaking artistic statement. Freddy connected the expression of Bronx, Brooklyn and Queens kids to the art movements of Soho. He made the visual side of hip hop more visible with every move he made, his immortalisation in Blondie's 'Rapture' perhaps the most memorable moment.

KURTIS MANTRONIK

Mantronik is the production figure who most emblematically straddles the move from the Old School to the New School eras, when hip-hop music started feeding in to all kinds of other growths – electro funk, techno, and eventually the ripples and shockwaves that would turn into drum and bass, jungle, even grime music. As Bambaataa had been influenced by Kraftwerk, so Mantronik, who formed the duo Mantronix with rapper MC Tee in 1984, was informed by influences far outside the normal sphere of hip-hop music. Krautrockers like Neu, as well as Old-School pioneers like Flash and Herc, found their way into the Mantronix sound. The result was a series of productions unlike anything that had happened in hip hop before, nigh-on shedding entirely the umbilicus back to traditional funk, with samples almost entirely erased in favour of spacious, heavily electronic textures that would massively influence a whole new generation of beat makers and producers.

Column 5

14 83 **W** Whodini	

15 84 **Rd** Run-DMC	20 80 **Rt** Roland TR-808	22 86 **Bb** Beastie Boys
16 86 **Sp** Salt n Pepa	21 87 **Eu** E-mu SP-1200	23 85 **Ll** LL Cool J
17 85 **Sc** Schoolly D		24 87 **Pe** Public Enemy
18 82 **Ff** Fab 5 Freddy		25 88 **Ep** EPMD
19 85 **Ku** Kurtis Mantronik		26 80 **Rs** Russell Simmons
		27 94 **Rr** Rick Rubin

It's impossible to tell the story of hip hop without pausing a moment to reflect on music technology. The hip-hop sound always rests on a crucial ambiguity.

The samples and textures hip hop deals in can be some of the warmest sounds in music – the drums, bass and timbre of sixties and seventies soul and funk music. But the technology hip hop uses is almost a sham of music making: the whole form is founded on using a machine of recreation (a turntable) as an actual creative device. The two most emblematic pieces of hardware hip hop has ever used both, in their way, crystallise that delicious dilemma, that tightrope between looseness/'feel' and machine-like tightness that hip hop's sound so engagingly steps on. They appear here as signposts both backward and forward in hip hop. The 808 is used all the way through from the Old School to the current period, and samplers, here represented by the E-mu SP-1200, are still being wrestled with in hip-hop studios worldwide. Kurtis Mantronik was perhaps one of the first and most innovative to use both.

ROLAND TR-808

Better drum machines were available. Initial reviews in 1980 were damning. In comparison to the concurrently launched Linn and Fairlight machines that used digital samples of real drums, the 808's sounds, its analogue-tone generation, seemed dated, a relic exposed by the far greater technical capabilities of its pricier rivals. There were more realistic drum machines. But who wants realism when for half the price you could sound like the future?

TR-808s, as DJs quickly discovered, were easier to program and could cut through the bedlam of hip-hop mixing like nothing else. A snare that chopped you like a scythe, a bass kick that hummed with depth and rattled your skull. Nothing sounds like an TR-808 because an

TR-808 isn't really set up to sound akin to anything. Its aim is not replication of the real, but the pure provision of rhythm, like a metronome.

At the precise moment that hip hop is abandoning its organic funk roots and seeking a way to imprint the unique artifice of DJing as its modus operandi, trying to build a bridge between live scratch-DJing and recorded sound, the TR-808 steps in like a beautifully ungainly idiot hero, in the right place at the right time in a way even the Roland engineers could never have predicted. Via Yellow Magic Orchestra the sound finds itself on Bam's 'Planet Rock' and hip hop is hooked.

Like the similarly revolutionary bass-generator the 303 (which would infect techno and house to such a huge degree in the late eighties and early nineties), the TR-808's pre-eminence in hip hop is down to reappropriation and abuse. The TR-808 was meant to be a studio tool, something intended purely for recording musicians to use to fill gaps left by absentee band-members and to record demos with. Put in a live scenario though, the TR-808 gives eighties rap a mighty sense of futurist power, a healthy sense of noise, a sound that hip hop still hasn't been able to shake. Kanye West's *808s & Heartbreak* is perhaps the most visible love letter to the machine that changed hip hop.

E-MU SP-1200

It's never the possibilities of music technology that dictate forward progress, rather it's the limitations, the barriers to imagination that they present and how artists go about butting their heads against those limitations and finding ingenious ways to transcend them. The SP-1200 is perhaps the most important bit of kit in hip-hop history, definitive of a whole decade of Golden-Age hip-hop production.

Before the SP-1200's release by E-mu systems in 1987 sampling and drum-machine technology had dictated the limitations of rap. Its predecessor, the SP-12, gave producers a couple of seconds of sampling time and some bone-crunching built-in drum beats, which corresponded perfectly with the brutal ways it was used by Schoolly D, the Beasties and others at the birth of the New School. By the time the SP-1200 replaced the SP-12 producers had a whopping 12 seconds of sampling time, crunchy digitised drum beats, and murky filtered bass-lines, all coming out of one cost-cutting machine. The sound of Golden-Age hip hop would hinge on those elements for a decade onwards.

The producers' creativity with those limitations is immense. In comparison with the supposedly infinite possibilities opened up by digital production after the nineties, the SP-1200 is almost laughably stunted. The much larger computational power put in our pockets and laptops and studios (the SP-1200 recorded in 12-bit audio; 128 or 320 were distant dreams) should've expanded the sonic possibilities of hip hop. But the struggle against the limitations of the SP-1200 and the unique combinations of sounds it could create within its limited palette made the period from 1988 to 1998 perhaps the most musically creative in hip hop, and led directly to the creation of some of the greatest art of the tail end of the century. Given all the time in the world to play with means hip-hop producers find it difficult to make timeless music. The SP-1200 forced it out of them, was a thing to play with rather than be bullied by – too often in modern hip-hop production you get the feeling the producer is simply guiding you round their mixing desk, expecting you to be goggle-eyed in awe. A guided tour around the SP-1200 would take five minutes. A machine of bliss creation.

Column 6

20 Rt 80 Roland TR-808	22 Bb 86 Beastie Boys	28 Bd 88 Big Daddy Kane
21 Eu 87 E-mu SP-1200	23 Ll 85 LL Cool J	29 Er 86 Eric B and Rakim
	24 Pe 87 Public Enemy	30 Sl 88 Slick Rick
	25 Ep 88 EPMD	31 Bz 88 Biz Markie
	26 Rs 80 Russell Simmons	32 Ma 87 Marley Marl
	27 Rr 94 Rick Rubin	

BEASTIE BOYS

Rick Rubin was familiar with the Beastie Boys in their punk-rock incarnation from when they played the warehouse at 171 Avenue A alongside Bad Brains and Black Flag, and supported Dead Kennedys and Misfits and other avatars of the growing hardcore punk scene at the legendary CBGBs club. He was truly entranced though by 'Cooky Puss' and the fact that the Beasties were, like him, punk rockers fascinated by hip hop, always checking out DJs and MCs after punk shows. With new names and a new direction (and shedding female member Katherine Shellenbach who 'didn't fit' Rubin's vision) Adam Horovitz, Adam Yauch and Michael Diamond became Ad-Rock, MCA and Mike D and started expanding the hip-hop elements of their punk-rock shows until the whole set was taken over by it. They took on Rubin as DJ Double-R, kitted themselves out in matching Puma or Adidas and went on to change the world.

When British Airways used a portion of 'Cooky Puss' without the Beastie Boy's permission in a TV ad they successfully sued the airline for $40,000 and used the money to rent a Chinatown apartment as a living space, rehearsal room and recording studio. Here they wrote the album *Licensed To Ill*, which wasn't released until late 1986 but as soon as it, and its smash hit singles ('(You Gotta) Fight For Your Right (To Party!)' and 'No Sleep Till Brooklyn'), were heard, something akin to nationwide madness occurred in the UK when the Beasties attempt to tour. Questions in Parliament, a rash of VW badge-theft... for the first time since the Sex Pistols there was a genuine worry that kids were being lured into depravity. That the Beasties could get through that moral panic to create two of the artistic high points of Golden-Age rap in *Paul's Boutique* and *Check Your Head* is testament to just how much the after-party mattered, how much they were learning about music all the time and what humility they naturally carried alongside their perceived arrogance. If you were idiotic enough to need proof that *anyone* from *any* background could have something unique to contribute to hip hop then the Beastie Boys provided it in spades, and gave us some of the most undimmed stupendous music and rhymes in the history of rap. They were spiritually one of the most hip-hop acts in hip hop.

LL COOL J

```
23        85
   LI
 LL Cool J
```

After Rubin somewhat foolishly put his NYU dorm-room address on the first record Def Jam brings out (T LA Rock's immense 'It's Yours') he's inundated with demos, and calls chasing up those demos. A demo with a Hollis, Queens postmark from a kid called Ladies Love Cool James stands out. When matched with Rubin's beats, J is too undeniable for Rubin to sell on – he wants to bring this music out himself, and persuades Russell Simmons to create a label with him to do just that, bypassing Profile, Tommy Boy and other likely outlets. Though 'It's Yours' featured the Def Jam logo it was really brought out by Arthur Baker's Partytime imprint, and thus Cool J's 'I Need A Beat' becomes the first Def Jam hip-hop release proper in 1984, a brilliantly tight, hard-hitting streetwise rap single that ends up selling 100,000 copies and launches Def Jam into the centre of the b-boy mindset. Cool J's voice is astonishingly confident for someone his age (only 16 when 'I Need A Beat' comes out), yet is natural, unaffected. All the insouciance of youth, the defiance, and yet there's something plaintive, touching and moving about Cool J's voice, even as he's spitting attitude at the cosmos. He's deeply deeply likeable from the off. Like Melle Mel he has that little bit 'extra' in his voice. Authority over himself and his expression. Untutorable, but unmistakable.

The album which follows, *Radio*, is, alongside DMC's *Raising Hell*, the state-of-the-art hip-hop release of the mid-eighties. Tracks like 'Radio' and 'Rock The Bells' are 1985's biggest anthems – 1987's *Bigger And Deffer* is precisely that (including the wonderfully sappy 'I Need

Love') and from then on Cool J's career takes a variety of interesting turns, his music never less than compelling, particularly on the majorly underrated later gems *Mama Said Knock You Out* and *14 Shots To The Dome*. Def Jam's first star, and in a lot of ways the rap star that most prefigured the mix of hardcore stance and pop-friendly versatility that every major rapper would have to cop ever since.

PUBLIC ENEMY

24 | 87
Pe
Public
Enemy

Public Enemy were, uniquely I think in the entire history of Western pop music, *perfect*. Not a band where you accept flaws but a band that highlighted pretty much every other band's flaws. A honed machine that tore like a juggernaut through your ideas of what hip hop – what music full stop – was capable of. The old debates – whether pop could sustain political narrative, whether there was any new noise to be made in music, whether pop could cause a revolution – all become moot points when confronted with Public Enemy because they took youth music to a height of sophistication, power and impact that's never been matched before or since.

Perfect in intent – hip hop not as dead end or constriction but as a launch pad into infinite knowledge and learning. Perfect in voice – there has never been a better match of persona and vocal tone than that of Flava Flav and Chuck D, each puncturing the other, each supporting the other. Perfect in sound – the Bomb Squad's productions for Public Enemy, from their debut album *Yo Bum Rush The Show*, through *It Takes A Nation Of Millions To Hold Us Back* and *Fear Of A Black Planet* and beyond (especially the massively underrated *Muse Sick-N-Hour Mess Age*) remain the most startling, stunningly detailed, exquisitely realised, astonishingly complex, brutally effective, endlessly delightful, infinitely rewarding music hip hop, or any genre from the eighties and nineties, ever gave us. Perfect in mindset – a recovery of hip hop's initial tenets (sound like anything, *say* anything), not so much pushing the edges of the envelope as shredding the fucker. Perfect stylistically – the way the logo, the looks, the S1Ws, the sleeves, everything fitted together to create sky-high art that utterly engulfed you.

Crucially for the future of hip hop Public Enemy revolutionised the way that hip hop saw itself, changed the way hip hop presented itself on stage, upped the ante on everything that followed. And while the press lost interest after that first flush of genius, for us fans Public Enemy kept on delivering, keep on delivering. Go see Public Enemy and I guarantee you won't see a more blissfully righteous, massively enjoyable gig in the rest of your life, or at least until you see the next Public Enemy show. Immortal and inspirational.

EPMD

Hip hop can always be understood in two ways – as it's enjoyed by its fans, and how the mainstream culture attempts to understand it. The former will lead you to good music, the latter will lead you to dominant official narratives in which crossover appeal and visibility, the easily understandable motifs of 'making it', will be all you'll garner. EPMD, like PE and the Beasties, were on Rush Management (Russell Simmons's management stable) but unlike those 'bigger' names, never caused outrage or started a riot. They're a reminder that hip hop, for the longest time, wasn't thought of by its fans as music in which success was purely quantified by media attention. It was music for outsiders. For hip-hop fans in the late eighties and early nineties, EPMD were the most consistently brilliant duo in rap, creating a succession of killer albums that sold huge amounts with minimum attention, sometimes for themselves, sometimes for others (do check out DAS EfX's *Dead Serious* for one of their finest oft-forgot productions). Albums that took hip-hop production deep inside itself, that focused above all on the listener-experience. This was not hip hop reaching out but hip hop reaching in, speaking to its own congregation, people for whom hip hop was less a force of extroversion than the chance to hide, to subsume yourself within a sound. James Brown was a sample-source that EPMD used a lot but it was also the heavy Roger Troutman and Zapp influences, the deeper funk influences, that were so tangible, long before other producers made the same connections elsewhere. Unlike later users of the P-funk sound like Dre, EPMD knew how to keep things excessive, smeared, blurry, heavy. Everything they made, from 1988's *Strictly Business* through to 1992's *Business Never Personal*, is essential.

RUSSELL SIMMONS

26		80
Rs		
Russell Simmons		

Hip hop's most immovable figure, a central protagonist all the way from hip hop's humble beginnings through to its current embedding as worldwide business, and yet Russell Simmons is one of the most mysterious people in rap. It's rare with Simmons that you can deduce whether he actually *likes* music. He can always see an opportunity, has a hustler's gift for talking those opportunities into realities, and making connections between people. But these are business and management skills. Like the sharpest pop entrepreneurs before him Simmons displays an almost ruthless ability to stay one step ahead of the game, to know his next two moves before he makes any move at all.

In hip hop's early years he worked hard to build a reputation as the fulcrum around which New York hip hop pivots. Unlike the almost comically vintage 'wear this'/'say this'/'you will record this' moves of the likes of Sylvie Robinson he encouraged artists to be themselves in order to make it an incredibly persuasive message. This gave Simmons an almost shamanic power among the crews and rappers he worked with, from Kurtis Blow through to Run-DMC and the Def Jam stable.

The fact he did a lot of this while being an entirely fucked up drug-hoover is incidental, although it does explain his later desire to push himself as some kind of pious Buddhist yogi. In his prime, the man was *crazed* but he made sure hip hop was expanding in a territorial sense. In 1985, the distribution deal for Def Jam was $600,000 with CBS Records; in 1999, Universal bought Def Jam for $120 million. By then, his own clothing line Phat Farm had grown to be a $140 million concern.

By taking the expressive art of an impoverished disenfranchised people and turning it into commerce Simmons, perhaps more than anyone else, made hip hop an all-pervasive element of American life. I think Simmons's suggestion that hip hop transformed America's perception of itself is entirely true but I'm sure that it was never the justification behind anything he did. His abandonment of rap could be seen as congruent with it slipping into the murky hands of mere money-makers with no knowledge of the history or culture of the music. But we should all be glad that, for a while, hip hop had a money-man batting for it who cared, who knew that for hip hop to move on it had to stop pretending to be pop and set itself up as a whole new kind of music.

RICK RUBIN

Hip hop is noisy music, it's transgressive music, it's accepting music; of course it would spin young Rick Rubin's propeller, and of course someone with such energy and vision would find a home in hip hop. Rubin's genius lies in his knowing that there are millions of kids like him, and in realising that hip hop, more than anything else, is the new rock'n'roll of the modern age.

The Beasties and Run-DMC had already been interpolating rock into their sound well before 'Walk This Way'. Everyone knows Rubin was in a punk band called the Pricks, thrown offstage after two songs at punk-rock mecca CBGBs for a pre-arranged brawl with the crowd. They were busted by Rubin's own dad who put on his Nassau cop uniform and drove two hours to NYC to do it. But his second band, Hose, is the more important band to hear because it makes you realise how influenced by post-punk Rubin was (especially Flipper, which was later reissued by the Infinite Zero imprint that Rubin set up with Henry Rollins). He loved bass music, noise music, and had the same ideas of hardcore self-sufficiency as Ian MacKaye. All of this would feed into Def Jam, the label that put out the first Hose single, which was run from Rubin's dorm room in NYU, a party room half kit and half dance floor where the Beastie Boys, LL Cool J and Run-DMC would regularly hang. When Special K's (Treacherous Three) elder bro T La Rock's hooked up with Zulu Nation DJ Jazzy Jay to unleash the awesome 'It's Yours' in 1984, Def Jam's first bona-fide smash, the seismic waves were sufficient to pull Russell Simmons and Rubin together. Within a couple of years, LL Cool J, the Beastie Boys and Public Enemy were all bringing out records emblazoned with the Def Jam logo, often featuring photography by old skate-punk pal Glen E. Friedman. If you can see that Def Jam logo spinning around your spindle, you know what you're in for: fun, aggression, something a little bit too much and scary.

Something was lost to Def Jam when Rubin sold his $2-billion share in 1996. It's not odd that Rubin got involved with hip hop, but I can't think of any other type of music that would let someone like Rubin exert so much control over the centre ground of a culture for so long. That's the thing with hip hop: it rewards the freaks and the geeks. It's accepting music.

Column 7

22 86 **Bb** Beastie Boys	28 88 **Bd** Big Daddy Kane	33 87 **Kr** KRS-One
23 85 **Ll** LL Cool J	29 86 **Er** Eric B and Rakim	34 88 **Um** Ultramagnetic MCs
24 87 **Pe** Public Enemy	30 88 **Sl** Slick Rick	35 89 **Du** Digital Underground
25 88 **Ep** EPMD	31 88 **Bz** Biz Markie	36 86 **Ji** Just-Ice
26 80 **Rs** Russell Simmons	32 87 **Ma** Marley Marl	37 81 **Rp** Robbins and Plotnicki
27 94 **Rr** Rick Rubin		38 90 **Lp** Large Professor

28   88

Bd

Big Daddy
Kane

BIG DADDY KANE

Perhaps the Juice Crew's brightest star, a rapper so damn good that legend has it even Rakim refused to battle him. Brooklynite BDK was pals with Biz Markie, wrote some of his most best-known raps and inked a deal with Cold Chillin' in 1987 for the debut single 'Raw'. Straight away you could tell Kane was something really special: his fast flow and totally authoritative voice were one thing, and could be admired as displaying real skills, but it was the persona behind the rhymes, the way BDK carried himself, that told you this man was gonna be a legend – he had star quality. That doesn't entail mere desire as it does now; it demands dignity, decorum, style and a confident and utterly seductive masculinity.

It was that mix between his absolute mastery of the mic, honed at Brooklyn block parties, and his look that made BDK so entrancing. In an era of sportswear and skinheads and jeans, BDK's flat-top, sharp suits and playa-style were an inspirational alternative. This didn't remove him from those fans, it brought them closer together, and made BDK an icon for a whole generation of rappers who wanted to return rap to a sense of theatre and drama. In a world of boys he gave himself a female-friendly smooth persona that reconnected rap with showmanship, swagger and spectacle (playing infamous Ladies Only shows at the Apollo). On wax, he was awesome too: the debut album *Long Live The Kane* was a record you learned by heart, not just the lines but the delivery and cadences. In 1988 only Rakim was beating BDK in terms of rappers you had to rewind and re-listen to in order to fully catch up with what they were saying.

Crucially, and oft-forgot, as a mentor he was always willing to let those who followed him in on the action. In 1990 BDK allowed a young Jay-Z to support him on his Chocolate City tour. Without a doubt the baby-faced nervy Jay learned an enormous amount from Kane. The definitive New-School rap star. I'm not sure we've seen one better since.

29   88

Er

Eric B and Rakim

ERIC B AND RAKIM

Rakim, in full flow, is the greatest rhymer in hip-hop history, 'Lyrics Of Fury' being, perhaps, his mightiest, moment. His voice, so fast a flow from mind to mouth, made you feel he could vanish himself into the infinite shadows of his own rhymes. Dense imagery, dizzying speed, Rakim was the rapper's rapper.

Eric B was a DJ on New York's WBLS radio station. He launched a search for 'New York's Top MC' to complement his turntable skills and Rakim answered the call. Eric B, handily, also shared an apartment with Marley Marl. Encouraged to use Marl's home studio the duo cut their first few tracks, impressing Russell Simmons so much they soon picked up a deal with Island Records. The superb debut *Paid In Full* propelled them into the charts via 'I Know You Got Soul' but it was on the next two albums, *Follow The Leader* and *Let The Rhythm Hit 'Em* that Eric B and Rakim pushed into uncharted space for rap. Not only was Eric B's production unique (although there are many uncredited producers on those albums including Large Professor) but Rakim was able to do things with his mouth that no other rapper could. He overstepped the limits of bars, lines, improvised like a jazz man over the strictures of four-four rhythm, frequently absconding his rhymes in mid-air until the beat could catch up, often seeming to explore a kind of polyrhythmic Eastern-style abstraction more akin to Thelonious Monk, John Coltrane or Miles Davis than anyone else in hip hop. There was something mesmerising about Rakim's writerly style, the way he structured rhymes in a totally free and unpredictable way, the way he could leave a word blazing in your memory and then pick up on it after several bars had passed. Listening to Rakim is an addictive, pure poetic thrill. Perhaps more than anyone, Rakim has a decent shout of being named as the greatest rapper of all time. Rappers still haven't caught up with Rakim.

SLICK RICK

Rick had already had an Old-School hit. Back when he was DJ Ricky D alongside Doug E. Fresh he'd hit the international charts with 'The Show' in 1983, performing on *Soul Train* in the States and *Top of the Pops* in the UK as part of Doug's Get Fresh Crew as well as contributing to the even more prized B-side 'La Di Da Di'. Rick was no stranger to the UK having been born in south-west London to Jamaican parents (picking up the eye-injury that necessitated his iconic eye-patch) and only moving to the Bronx in 1976 aged 11. The Brit-accent percolated into Rick's rapping, unmistakably, giving him the simultaneous air of a Victorian guttersnipe and an uppity aristocrat.

What was remarkable was how many other voices he could take on, how he could tell stories from multiple perspectives using those multiple voices. He was also perhaps the funniest MC out there. Rick was self-deprecating, nonchalant in his delivery. He never free-styled, he wrote carefully constructed narratives and enunciated them clearly but shot them through with sing-song cadences and musical playfulness. Breath was no limit as he'd use punch-ins of multiple tracks to create a collage of voices that diffused identity. At no point did he seem concerned that his style was utterly isolated in rap and that's perhaps why he's one of the most heralded voices in hip hop.

Every rapper who's ever been worried that what they're bringing might be too oddball, too off the wall, too strange to be palatable, should take strength and conviction from Slick Rick, the original hip-hop maverick and proof that the New School could and would sustain totally new narratives for hip hop.

BIZ MARKIE

'The clown-prince of hip hop' conjures a court-jester, certainly not someone pivotal to the progression of a culture. Biz Markie is more important than that sobriquet suggests, or his status as 'comic relief' in the Juice Crew would imply. Of course, the hapless oaf would end up dropping hip hop deep in the doo-doo, and end up having far more of a lasting effect on rap than even he could have envisaged. And, of course, end up forgiven because up to that point he'd been one of the funniest, most touching and personable talents in rap.

Rap is funny. It can be funny in ways that other music can't manage. It can be free with its timing and structures in a way that suits comedy. It can make every line a feed and every closing phrase a punch line. Biz was a master at everything – DJing, rapping, beat-boxing – and the albums he created between 1988 and 1991 for Cold Chillin' are some of the most joyous cartoons hip hop ever gave us. *Goin' Off* gave Marl a chance to make his production as varied and funfair-esque as Markie's stories and the self-produced *The Biz Never Sleeps* even made Biz an unlikely star with the ace, moving, loser-rap hit 'Just A Friend'. It was the third album, *I Need A Haircut*, where the clown made his biggest pratfall. Blatantly using Gilbert O'Sullivan's 'Alone Again (Naturally)' on the track 'Alone Again' wasn't a smart move, given Biz's profile. O'Sullivan's label sued Warner Bros. Warner Bros disputed the copyright claim by O'Sullivan's label but admitted they had looked for permission, thus proving they knew they were breaking the law. Sampling's prevalence in hip hop at the time was no defence. Judge Duffy of the District Court of South New York began his ruling by quoting the Bible, 'Thou shalt not steal'. This first ruling that sampling was copyright infringement sent out the message that from here on in, hip hop would have to seek permission before using samples. The sampladelic textures of Bomb Squad or Native Tongues productions would never be heard again. From 1991 onwards, hip hop has had to find new ways to make a noise. Interpolation, just as Sugar Hill Records and Enjoy Records had done, was one way: paying the songwriters, not the label, and using replayed versions of what you'd previously have been able to simply thieve. Obscurantism was another way, digging in crates so deep you could be sure no one would chase you, and then twisting those samples out of shape until they were unrecognisable anyway. Hip hop would spend the next decade working out its own methods. It led to some of the most creative, groggiest, shiniest music it had ever made. Biz stayed sheepish. His next album was called *All Samples Cleared*. Funny guy.

MARLEY MARL

32	87
Ma	
Marley Marl	

Marley Marl was a smart assistant to some of hip hop's most pivotal names, interning for Arthur Baker and experimenting with his cutting-edge equipment to create massively popular mix-tapes in his native Queens, assisting Mr Magic on WBLS Radio and always learning. Marl's use of sampled break-beats on MC Shan's 'The Bridge' in 1985 was fresh and new, and the way he combined those filched and reprogrammed beats with synthetic TR-808 rhythm became pretty much the model of hip-hop production for the next half a decade. Starting out with way-more electro-based Mantronik-style productions for Spoonie Gee on Tuff City Records, by 1985, on his own label Cold Chillin' and with his own army of rappers the Juice Crew, Marl was shedding the overtly electronic elements of his sound, aiming for an altogether funkier, warmer, more organic sample-based sound on early productions for Shan, Big Daddy Kane, Biz Markie, Roxanne Shanté, Kool G Rap and DJ Polo, and Masta Ace. Finding the choicest drum beats and samples from the 1970s and 1960s funk to flesh out his tracks, meant that he decreased hip hop's reliance on thin metallic drum-machine beats and lent hip-hop production a fresh impact that put all Marley Marl productions a cut above most hip hop at the time. Every super-producer in hip hop since – Premier, Pete Rock, Large Pro, the RZA – has in some way borrowed and stolen a little of Marley Marl's magic. If you're crate-digging, a Marley Marl Production is still an immortal seal of quality.

Column 8

28 **88** **Bd** Big Daddy Kane	**33** **87** **Kr** KRS-One	**39** **86** **It** Ice-T
29 **86** **Er** Eric B and Rakim	**34** **88** **Um** Ultramagnetic MCs	**40** **88** **Nw** N.W.A.
30 **88** **Sl** Slick Rick	**35** **89** **Du** Digital Underground	**41** **87** **Ee** Eazy-E
31 **88** **Bz** Biz Markie	**36** **86** **Ji** Just-Ice	**42** **89** **Gb** Geto Boys
32 **87** **Ma** Marley Marl	**37** **81** **Rp** Robbins and Plotnicki	**43** **86** **Jh** Jerry Heller
	38 **90** **Lp** Large Professor	**44** **88** **Dd** Dr Dre

KRS-ONE

There was something messianic, wide-eyed, about Lawrence 'Krsna' Parker aka KRS-One, an epic self-righteousness and a hippy soul that underscored his hardcore pretensions. An ex-weed-running, Beatles-quoting vegetarian, it always seemed that Parker was looking for beef where there was none. He was initially confrontational when meeting his homeless-shelter counsellor and future DJ, Scott Sterling (DJ Scott La Rock, whose fatal shooting in 1987 was perhaps hip hop's first major casualty of war). As KRS-One, Parker was seemingly always on edge, about to be triggered, like any cornered youngster who sees no future, or who feels that the system is dedicated to shutting them down. In his crew Boogie Down Productions, Parker never seemed in the mood to placate anyone, rather his tone was always inflammatory, demanding, daring you to answer. Boogie Down Productions were obsessed with realness. They were 10 years into hip-hop history and already claims over hip-hop origins and a desire to take the art form 'back' to what it once was were everywhere. The Bridge Wars that kicked off between KRS-One's Boogie Down Productions posse and Marley Marl's Juice Crew were founded on a falsehood, a deliberate misreading of MC Shan's 'The Bridge' as if it were positing some Queensbridge origin-myth for hip hop (a feud that wouldn't die until 2007). The 'South Bronx' single and *Criminal Minded* LP that followed in 1987 still sound lividly mean, thanks in large part to Scott La Rock and Ultramagnetic MC producer Ced Gee's brutal production, and KRS-One's hunger, something amplified by the heavy reggae/dancehall influence that seemed to suffuse through those early Boogie Down Productions tracks. A heavy influence on future gangsta-rap in both lyrical focus and style (*Criminal Minded* is one of the first hip-hop albums to feature guns on the cover) as well as the free-floating 'collective' nature of Boogie Down Productions itself, whose massive cast of characters would go on to be dissed and disowned on 1992's spectacularly bitchy *Sex and Violence*. Note – KRS-One was responsible, beyond Boogie Down Productions, for one of the greatest comeback singles in hip-hop history: 'Rappaz R N Dainja' in 1995.

ULTRAMAGNETIC MCS

The Ultramagnetics were utterly unique, though hip-hop mavericks ever since have subconsciously touched the hem of their fabulous garments. Formed around the nexus of producer Ced Gee and rapper Kool Keith, Ultramags also featured Moe Love and TR Love and came together at DeWitt Clinton High School in the Bronx.

Critical Beatdown, their masterpiece, is crucial to understanding how far hip-hop production had developed by 1988 but, more importantly, it's Ultramags' lyrical response to their times that was so revolutionary and suggestive. Kool Keith and Ced Gee wrote and produced music that reflected a desire to escape their reality, to talk in the kind of stream-of-consciousness, occasionally lucid, way of any reasonable dust-smoker from the hood. Pulling in sci-fi, UFOs, B-movie monsters, old-time Hollywood – *anything* into his flow – Kool Keith used words no other rapper used, and used them not just for the phonetic delight they'd create but for the strange metaphorical trails the listener would end up stranded on, something aided by his oddball enunciation, his lunatic-in-authority voice. Similarly, Ced Gee's production and beats were fast and hard and lurid and freaky in a way that no other hip hop could get close to (at least until later crews like De La Soul could fully explore their Ultramags-fandom on their own records). Ced Gee's beats didn't just move forward, they moved around the mix. Every element of UMCs' music was elastic, where on BDP's *Criminal Minded* Gee's (uncredited) production had to be based around the essentially hardcore and heavy subjects and style of KRS's rhyming, on *Critical Beatdown*, his unique sample sources and feel could be twisted around a lyrical vision as wide-open and bug-eyed as his own. The result is one of the high-points of New-School rap, one that was picked up on not just by a legion of contemporary fans in hip hop (impossible to hear Bomb Squad productions without hearing how influenced by Ced Gee they were), but by those who'd end up making the big beat and trip-hop and instrumental dance music of the nineties. Both Keith and Ced haven't really needed to work since the mechanical royalties for the Prodigy's 'Out Of Space' and 'Smack My Bitch Up' started rolling in. The tracks used chunks of UMCs' 'Critical Beatdown' and 'Give The Drummer Some' respectively. Do not progress beyond eighties hip hop without hearing *Critical Beatdown*.

DIGITAL UNDERGROUND

Before Tim Dog took on an entire seaboard with 'Fuck Compton', before Tupac and Biggie Smalls ever sniped at each other, before anyone even talked about hip hop in terms of what coast it came from, no one gave a fuck about the fact that Digital Underground weren't from New York, that they had, in fact, originated from Oakland, California. Although, in truth, Oakland had percolated into their sound and vision.

There was something decidedly rebellious and subversive about what Digital Underground did, something sophisticated and profane. Perhaps more than any other crew Digital Underground were a true modern P-funk, replete with catchphrases, characters, albums that told stories that hung together and only expanded the intrigue, band members that took on multiple identities. Greg Jacobs who, as Shock G and Humpty Hump, would play both the straight front-man and wise-cracking Groucho-style comedian in the crew (as seen on their breakthrough hit 'The Humpty Dance'), had already led multiple lives by the time Digital Underground came together in Oakland in the late eighties. Equal parts Pakistani, Indian, Jewish, Puerto Rican and Trinidadian,

Jacobs had bummed around the country for years playing and learning about music before putting together the Digital Underground collective in 1988. The conceptual depth behind their work relied on his playfulness with identity, a sense that posse cuts could be conversational and experimental as well as confrontational. *Sex Packets*, their debut LP, remains one of the greatest debuts in all rap. It is one of the finest concept albums ever, lyrically one of the sharpest, funniest and freakiest suites of skulduggery hip hop's ever given us and, musically, an album that prefigures G-funk by a good three years but gets nowhere near the props it should. It's tragic that Digital Underground are remembered chiefly for being the first crew to feature Tupac. Don't remember them that way.

36	86
Ji	
Just-Ice	

JUST-ICE

Most rappers can snarl and spit and bark and bite but you know in real life they'd be pussycats. Perhaps the scariest rapper of all was Just-Ice. Everything you heard from, and heard about, this avatar of gangsta-rap scared the bejesus out of you. That he was locked up aged 12 and ended up in the same homeless shelter as KRS-One and Scott La Rock. That he used to be a bouncer in DC's hardest-core punk clubs, where he'd back up threats by waving pistols in people's faces. That he knocked out Cold Chillin' boss Len Fichtelberg over a few hundred dollars. That he had the balls to claim in print interviews that Run-DMC were all crack dealers. That when 'The Bridge' wars were popping off he personally went looking for Blaq Poet armed with a shotgun after Poet had declared that 'Just-Ice will melt'. That he turned up on photographer Janette Beckman's doorstep holding a kitten he'd just adopted and christened 'Money Clip'. That he's the sole reason Unique Studios in Times Square installed bullet-proof glass in their reception and lobby area. At all times Just-Ice seemed like he could kick off in an instant.

It's that palpable sense of genuine menace that makes *Back To The Old School*, his 1986 debut, such an undimmed classic in rap aggravation. Brutal beats, brutal rhymes and the ever-present threat that if you questioned this guy in any way he'd punch you in the windpipe and then use his mouthful of gold teeth to bite your face off. Along with Kool G Rap, he was, perhaps New York's most unsettling New-School MC. The original hip-hop hard man.

CORY ROBBINS AND STEVE PLOTNICKI

Having made its break and seen the world, the last thing hip hop needed in the mid-eighties was 'interested parties' like Sylvie and Bobby Robinson. Although Def Jam, the imprint and legend, remain enormous, in its infancy it was a chaotic label that mirrored the chaotic lifestyles of its two founders, and was run by the professionalism of its artists and their associates. Profile Records, founded by Cory Robbins and Steve Plotnicki, was far more definitive of what made a great early hip-hop label because their association with rap was an accident rather than a manoeuvre, and it was most assuredly hands-off rather than hands-on.

Like Tommy Silverman originally intended with Tommy Boy, Profile was really set up as a dance-music label and its two co-founders were certainly not hip-hop fans. Hip hop was seen by Profile as the tougher end of what they put out, but soon it was that tougher end that wound up keeping their company afloat and playing the bills. For a long time, one-off hip-hop hits was how b-boys grew familiar with that Profile logo. Records like Dr Jeckyll and Mr Hyde's Tom Tom Club-ripping 'Genius Rap' or Rob Base and DJ E-Z Rock's worldwide chart smash 'It Takes Two'.

As an indie, Profile knew that albums were not the only game in town. They thrived on 12-inch culture and knew how to properly promote 12 inches through the clubs, live shows and radio. They also knew how to promote music on the street, networking promoters with managers and artists in a way that didn't need a big industry structure to create interest. Bigger labels, later on, would learn, and create small subsidiaries and imprints to build this kind of grassroots loyalty (the best example being Universal/K-Tel's creation of the Priority imprint). In the mid-eighties only labels like Profile, run often by moneyed white suburbanite dabblers in underground culture, had the smarts to build from the ground up, buy up what hot local labels they could, and get themselves the hottest roster in hip hop. Run-DMC, the fantastic Special Ed, O.C.'s wonderful *Word... Life*, Smoothe da Hustler (the extraordinary 'Broken Language'), Camp Lo (the exquisite 'Luchini'), Nine and Poor Righteous Teachers would all find a home on Profile. If only hip-hop labels today could be so unobtrusive, admit they don't really understand hip hop, and leave it to its own devices like Profile did.

LARGE PROFESSOR

A breaker turned DJ, who learned young of the value of finding the choicest cuts. Large Pro's tutors in hip hop, who would include Ultramagnetic MCs' Paul C, would give him lists of records to seek out, always with the caveat that he'd never be able to find all of them. He accepted the challenge and always, throughout his productions, laced the music with textures and elements that no one else did and incorporated his deep knowledge of jazz-funk into his grooves. The SP-1200, as introduced to him by Paul C, absolutely blew his mind with the ease of use and capabilities of quickly creating killer tracks. He'd become immersed in it, stacking up track after track. Because of the depth of his musical learning and knowledge, Large Pro tracks were always worth seeking out.

After leaving Main Source soon after the release of *Breaking Atoms*, he'd go on to perform vital production work for Slick Rick, Eric B and Rakim (stepping in after Paul C passed on during the creation of *Let The Rhythm Hit 'Em*), the unmissable Kool G Rap and DJ Polo (the

superb *Wanted: Dead Or Alive* set) as well as inspiring
fellow crate-digger Pete Rock to new heights by finding
the horn-loop that would be the basis for 'T.R.O.Y'.

The crucial thing about the era of producers who
came up in the late eighties and early nineties was a
sense of shared endeavour. Large Pro, Finesse, Pete Rock
and Diamond D would be in the same shops, hunting the
same racks, helping each other out in digging out the
best loops, the rarest grooves. Mainly remembered now
as the man who gave Nas his first cameo, and then built
much of the monster that would be *Illmatic*, make sure
you seek out pretty much everything imprinted with the
Xtra P touch.

Column 9

		45 De **De** De La Soul 89

33 **Kr** KRS-One 87	39 **It** Ice-T 86	46 **Tq** A Tribe Called Quest 89
34 **Um** Ultramagnetic MCs 88	40 **Nw** N.W.A. 88	47 **Ju** Jungle Brothers 88
35 **Du** Digital Underground 89	41 **Ee** Eazy-E 87	48 **Bl** Black Sheep 91
36 **Ji** Just-Ice 86	42 **Gb** Geto Boys 89	49 **Kd** Kool DJ Red Alert 86
37 **Rp** Robbins and Plotnicki 81	43 **Jh** Jerry Heller 86	50 **Pp** Prince Paul 89
38 **Lp** Large Professor 90	44 **Dd** Dr Dre 88	

ICE-T

Gangsta-rap at its best balances the dualities of criminal life, the confidence and the paranoia, the fatalism and the fixations, the gang-strength and the lonely death. Ice, as Just-Ice and Schoolly D had done before him, did exactly that. The single 'Six In The Morning' and *Rhyme Pays,* Ice's LP debut in 1986, first alerted the world to this new, yet almost elderly voice in rap but it was the album that followed, *Power,* that first properly gave us the mix between street-level nitty-gritty and soul-on-ice psychological analysis that made Ice's contribution to hip hop so unique.

Ice's media-friendliness, his flexibility of taste and his sheer busy-ness might make hip-hop fans balk at his presence here but he's a pivotal figure in rap, indicating how hip hop was going to swing away from its Nuyorican centrism and start exploring the corners of its home continent, instrumental in breaking New York's grip over the culture and expanding it out to the Pacific, just as he had been relocated from New Jersey to Crenshaw. Ice was smart enough to keep his history shady, hinted at (you knew that he'd travelled in and out of the army and seemed to have dabbled in robbery, drug-dealing and pimping like his hero Iceberg Slim). You knew, or at least were convinced, that criminality was not something he was merely observing. On the albums *The Iceberg/ Freedom Of Speech* and his masterpiece *O.G. Original Gangster* Ice would also expand rap's reach into rock audiences, white audiences, and was always keen to seek those fertile grounds of cross-fertilisation between punk and metal (which he was a major fan of) and hip hop. At crucial moments when hip hop was in danger of slotting neatly along the margins of mainstream culture, Ice returned it to outrage, rebellion and always had a keen political edge to his songs – fiercely anti-conservative, fiercely free-speech, fiercely anti-police. *Power, Iceberg* and *O.G.* remain hugely enjoyable records for the wit, the beats, the variety of the music and the dangerous sense that for a while Ice-T was as close as hip hop ever got to a renaissance star.

N.W.A.

No one ever complains about opera or Shakespeare where sex, death, incest, murder, rape and disembowelment often feature. Those audiences wouldn't get 'affected'. By the late eighties *everyone* was complaining about hip hop. Inevitably, as a marginal, working-class, young people's music it was bound to find itself the target of panicky middle-class moral arbiters. The most visible of these, Tipper Gore and her fellow Washington Wives, took their incorruptible outrage with the tides of explicit filth being served up by US rap, metal and punk music all the way to a congressional hearing. With the only stout defence being provided by musicians themselves, and industry body the RIAA striking compromises that made no one happy, the lasting result of the Parents' Music Resource Centre's agitation for an age-rating system for music was the infamous 'Tipper Sticker', the 'Parental Advisory: Explicit Lyrics' emblem that came to save mainstream retailers from blow-back, and destroy indie labels and artists that relied on distribution to mainstream stores, if they dared to continue putting out explicit content.

Although Gore's on-going wars with Luke Skyywalker's inordinately rude 2 Live Crew ultimately nearly broke that crew apart, rap music, perhaps even more than metal and punk, massively benefited from the essentially useless warning sticker. As a kid in a record store, the 'Explicit Lyrics' sticker was like a beacon, promising filth and transgressions and assuring you that if you bought this, something in it would make you laugh, gasp, pump it loud until your parents banged on the door. The congressional hearings about hip hop continue to occur every now and then and will come, variously, from the NRA, Republican conservatives and bleeding-heart liberals alike. Outrage, scapegoating, the earmarking of hip hop as the soundtrack to a generation's moral decay – these will always benefit hip hop massively.

Outrage fuelled the rise of N.W.A. but once that had run out, it became evident how precarious their avowed 'importance' was. By any reasonable, statistical or financial criteria N.W.A. are 'important'. They were not the first gangsta-rappers; I'd say that honour goes to Schoolly D and Just-Ice. They were not the first West Coast rappers to hit big; Ice-T definitely got there first. And crucially, their debut LP *Straight Outta Compton* is not a classic. Its 'iconic' status has been attained due to the laziness of those who want the transition from New-School rap into gangsta-rap to follow neat understandable lines of upheaval. It's actually (drum roll) a *crap* album, about three good tracks and a whole load of filler and, as such, provides a good template for much that would follow from the West Coast, the patchiness and inconsistency and overratedness that Tupac would make his own. N.W.A. are considered important by mainly white cultural arbiters and curators because they pulled a lot of white boys into hip hop, wannabe gangstas and middle-class fantasists, who had no understanding of the music's history, loved the easy choruses and simplistic wordplay and were overjoyed that middle-class rappers in the studio were willing to play gangsta roles for their entertainment. *Efil4zaggin*, the follow up, was actually better but in comparison to what else was going on in hip hop at the time we're still clutching at straws. The times were too great to be summated by the overrated crock that is *Straight Outta Compton* – from here on in we have to watch what we call 'important' and always ask whether we're anointing artefacts with importance because of their inherent worth or because of the buzz-storm of bullshit that's been successfully conjured out of them. In N.W.A.'s case it's definitely the latter, and for all the anti-establishment rhetoric, the deep conventionality and conservatism of what they represent still lingers, that tilting of interest away from the music and towards rap as wrestling-style 'entertainment', an endless dizzying parade of thuggery, beefs, dissing and other irrelevancies. In that sense they were 'important'.

EAZY-E

As a hip-hop fan I was massively aggravated by the undue attention West Coast hip hop got, the way its criminal tropes became the only story. Its rise seemed predicated on the fact that archetypes and stereotypes were West Coast hip hop's stock in trade. It was a direct contradiction to East Coast hip hop's expansion and elaboration of black identity and black music. I make an exception for Eazy-E though because his early work is so damn likeable, starting of course with 'Boyz-N-The-Hood'. Eazy at the time didn't think he was a rapper but the New York groups he tried to foist the Ice Cube-penned track on to couldn't cope with the West Coast terminology of it, and he eventually was persuaded by Dre to step up to the mic. The album that followed in 1988, *Eazy-Duz-It*, is an ensemble piece – ghostwriting duties go to MC Ren, Ice Cube and D.O.C. (whose *No One Can Do It Better* is another Ruthless release that far surpasses *Straight Outta Compton*). They gave Eazy raps that suited his persona as an ex-drug dealer now dealing in sonic crack via his own label, but crucially it was Eazy's voice that really set *Eazy-Duz-It* apart. By 1988 we were used to the stentorian in rap, the declamatory sounds of an MC in charge and bossing the mic and the crowd. What was so joyous about Eazy was not that he sounded like the leader of a gang or a front-man. Rather he sounded like the dangerous snarly short-arse at the back of the gang, petulant, childish sometimes, always with something to prove, always even more of a uncontrollable hooligan than his beefier more measured confederates. There's a puerile sense of total juvenile delinquency to *Eazy-Duz-It*, and it relies entirely on Eazy's high-pitched, hysterical flow and his confidence in his own persona. This was brat rap, as self-deprecating as it was self-assured, one of Ruthless's first albums and probably its best. Eazy's ensuing problems with both Ruthless and the AIDS virus that took his life far too soon in 1995 make him far more of a tragic figure for me than Tupac or Biggie. Never forget him.

GETO BOYS

42 89
Gb
Geto Boys

Crucially, Geto Boys came from Houston and that Texan heat will fry your brain. Geto Boys started out with a completely different line up to the one that would become infamous. Jukebox, DJ Ready Red and Johnny C made up the bulk of the crew, with the pint-sized Bushwick Bill merely the dancer. When Johnny C and Jukebox quit, former Rap-A-Lot artists Scarface and Willie D were drafted in by the record company. In 1990 David Geffen refused to distribute the group's debut LP *Grip It! On That Other Level* because the lyrics were so gloriously offensive. This became a perfect marketing tool for Rick Rubin's Def America imprint, which remixed and repackaged the album as *The Geto Boys*, replete with family-fave murder-necrophilia anthem 'Mind Of A Lunatic'. The group left Geffen for Rap-A-Lot and mayhem soon ensued. Bushwick Bill was shot in the eye and partially blinded by his girlfriend after threatening their child, an incident immortalised on the sleeve of the follow up LP *We Can't Be Stopped*, with a gruesome shot of Bill being pushed through the hospital with Scarface and Willie D. *We Can't Be Stopped* is a stunning record, the occasional moments of gallows-insight touched on by their debut reaching a full revelatory denouement on tracks like the startling 'Mind Playing Tricks On Me'. The music was crepuscular, smeared with molten neon, and could never have come from New York. It detailed an entirely new and unique kind of gangsta doom. This was paranoia breaking out across the body, across the voice, satanic dreams and visions made flesh. Geto Boys's music unfolds like a crack-ravaged frightmare of half-seen shadows and peripheral phantoms, always haunted by a murky lurking horror. Unlike everything else called gangsta in the late eighties and early nineties, it's music truly without redemption, only dread. Music that perfectly details the socio-psychological damage a decade of Reaganomics had wreaked in America's underbelly.

JERRY HELLER

Ruthless Records was one of the most successful start-up record companies in the history of black music but who cares about that, eh? Who wanted to shoot who? Talk of Ruthless Records nearly always quickly turns into a list of who hated who and who wanted who dead, mainly because the vast bulk of Ruthless's catalogue is justly forgotten and rarely retrieved from the racks, partly because nothing turns on a mainstream culture more than tales of internecine black-on-black corporate hostility, which nicely shores up the stereotype that business-management is somehow 'beyond' black people, and conveniently ignores the fact that many of Ruthless's difficulties were because of the intransigence of its boss, Jerry Heller.

Ruthless's problems start with N.W.A. wanting recompense from Heller, who set up the label with Eazy-E and seemed to be living the mansioned high-life as they were stuck in tour vans and cheap hotels and living in the same apartments they always had. *Straight Outta Compton* was the label's first LP release and went multi-platinum; singles and solo albums from Eazy-E also did phenomenally well but none of the capital generated seemed to be making it into the pockets of the artists. Ice Cube, perhaps N.W.A.'s one convincing MC and writer bar Eazy-E, left and signed a solo deal with Ruthless's distributors Priority. The remaining members inked solo deals with Ruthless and the building hostility between roster and label bosses kept growing. Ruthless was still producing hits, from Above the Law to Bone

Thugs-n-Harmony but the writing was on the wall when even Eazy started to realise he was being jacked by Heller. N.W.A. producer Dr Dre in particular felt stung by how his hard work for the group was incommensurate with his earnings. His friends, D.O.C. and Suge Knight encouraged him to jump ship and lubricate his escape by taking hired goons with baseball pats and lead pipes round to Heller's office to insist that Dre be freed from his contract. It worked, and Death Row Records is the result. From then on, Ruthless's demise was assured. You'll note that at no point here have I mentioned any of the music that came out on Ruthless. I've mentioned silly-boy games, one-upmanship and bun-fights. This is the way the story turns when LA gets involved. Show business. In a sense, no different from the years of Sugar Hill and Enjoy. With extra violence and mayhem.

DR DRE

Dre's often lambasted as an overrated producer but I think the mistake people make is in thinking he cares about hip hop. I'm not sure he ever has: Dre is far more interested in making pop music. And at that, he's a genius, good enough to give Tupac his one good moment on 'California Love'. When he was DJing in LA clubs like Eve After Dark in the eighties with his World Class Wreckin' Cru, he'd pride himself on jamming old Motown, Supremes, Temptations, Martha Reeves in amid the electro and breaking hits that formed the bulk of his playlist. He loves pop, always, loves the lustre of its sound and loves the idea of a production line, the ultimate control it affords the producer. He wanted to be a one-man Motown for the twenty-first century. As it turned out, he became Victor Kiam.

The backroom of Eve After Dark was where Dre, DJ Yella and Lonzo Williams would record demos, learn turntable techniques, learn production. Seven out of the eight albums Dre produced for Ruthless went platinum. His best work for N.W.A. (especially the underrated

Efil4zaggin) was what saved that group from mediocrity. Released by the barrel of a gun to go play on Death Row Records he refined and perfected his sound into G-funk, slower and slinkier than P-funk, dodging sample clearance by interpolation, music that attained the perfect sunkissed Californian pace of a heartbeat, a car wheel, a sun-struck sigh. *The Chronic* was the album that created the West Coast sound of the early nineties and made that sound mainstream. *Doggystyle* was another major leap forward, light years beyond the chaos and amateurism of N.W.A. For the next four years Dre's sound would dominate pop. Increasingly unhappy at Death Row, he left in 1996 to create his own label, Aftermath, declaring gangsta-rap dead. Death Row's implosion in 1997 proved him right. His launching of Eminem and his comeback album, the superb *2001*, saw him back at the top.

Every move, including his creation and selling of his Beats headphones brand, has been ruthlessly calculated. He doesn't need a musical legacy now.

Golden
Age

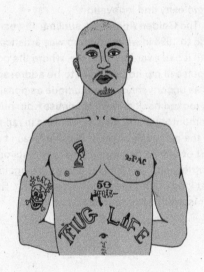

Oft yearned for by ageing b-boys and b-girls as a lost epoch of innocence in hip hop, really what the Golden Age can be defined by is not necessarily just the quality of hip hop that was created but the sheer variety of it, and the sense that you were hearing an art form being conjured into new spaces every time you tapped into it.

All bets were off in the Golden Age – the hardcore constrictions of the Old School and New School eras could be jettisoned – any subject matter was admissible, from the brutally violent to the hysterically comic, from the trippy and psychedelic to the most vérité and documentarian. Musically too, the Golden Age was an era in which sampling hit a dizzying new depth of layered complexity and innovation.

The Golden Age was a sublime 10-year period from 1988 to 1998 in which hip hop was artistically more free than it had ever been before, where the commercial impulse in hip hop seemed to be addressed by trying to be as unconventional and unique as possible. Inevitably, it's looked back on with fondness from our current promontory of identikit sameyness in rap music. But don't let the name blind you: it certainly wasn't all golden. Part of the Golden Age mythology rests on it being irretrievable: 'We'll never see its like again.' Well, with that kind of attitude of course we won't. Still, a goldmine of inspiration for rap music, always.

Column 10

	45 **De** 89 De La Soul	
39 **It** 86 Ice-T	46 **Tq** 89 A Tribe Called Quest	51 **Gs** 91 Gang Starr
40 **Nw** 88 N.W.A.	47 **Ju** 88 Jungle Brothers	52 **P** 92 Pharcyde
41 **Ee** 87 Eazy-E	48 **Bl** 91 Black Sheep	53 **Ms** 91 Main Source
42 **Gb** 89 Geto Boys	49 **Kd** 86 Kool DJ Red Alert	54 **Km** 91 KMD
43 **Jh** 86 Jerry Heller	50 **Pp** 89 Prince Paul	55 **Dp** 89 DJ Premier
44 **Dd** 88 Dr Dre		

45		89
	De	
De La Soul		

DE LA SOUL

For all the musical richness of the New School there was always something a little monochrome, deliberately so, about hip hop until De La Soul. They were New Yorkers relocated in Long Island, and Posdnuos and Trugoy the Dove had known each other since the early eighties, and while attending Amityville High School had hooked up with Pasemaster Mase. Doing the rounds of various crews before forming De La Soul in 1985, Mase met a local DJ Prince Paul Huston of Stetsasonic, who started mentoring the teenagers. Securing them a deal with Tommy Boy, Stetsasonic's label, resulted in 'Plug Tunin' becoming an underground smash in 1988, bringing De La Soul into contact with the Jungle Brothers who in turn welcomed them into their Native Tongues stable. Though a neat fit, there's a depth to Prince Paul's production that separated De La Soul from their contemporaries. Their epochal debut *3 Feet High And Rising*, though sold with that gruesome by-line 'daisy-age soul', is more often the sound of Paul destroying the conventions of hip hop with a lunatic glee. It's a zenith for pre-sample-clearance hip hop. The sense of anarchy and fun, in contrast to so much heaviness in rap at the time, is what made De La Soul a refreshing alternative, and also amenable to those white pop fans for whom hip hop had already gone 'too far'. Paul's production was gloriously irreverent, breakneck, light-speed psyche-pop. Problem was that as a document *3 Feet High* is exhaustive and a dead end. By putting everything from Steely Dan to Curiosity Killed the Cat up for grabs it was as close as hip hop got in the late eighties to simply assimilating itself into pop music. Paul's restlessness made for a great album, an ear-popping album but couldn't sustain itself beyond that flashpoint.

The tag 'hippie rap' grew wearisome for the trio, sample-clearance lawsuits from sixties psyche-pop band the Turtles didn't help, and most hip-hop fans now dig into the far deeper, far darker post-fame albums that De La Soul made, including the bitter and bleak *De La Soul Is*

Dead, the woozy and garish *Buhloone Mindstate* and the post-Prince Paul hard-hitter *Stakes Is High* (for a similarly engrossing move from populism to pariah-status check Dream Warriors's progress from *And Now The Legacy Begins* to the superb *Subliminal Simulation*). No denying though that the 'daisy-age' summer of 1989 retains a warm fuzzy place in most hip-hop fans' memories, when 'Eye Know' and 'The Magic Number' and 'Say No Go' and 'Me Myself And I' were everywhere.

A TRIBE CALLED QUEST

In 1989–90, De La Soul's years of dominance, you couldn't get away from the 'daisy age', from the mainstream press telling you that De La Soul had changed rap for ever. As a rap fan, you were inevitably looking the other way and listening instead to A Tribe Called Quest's *People's Instinctive Travels*. In 1991, as gangsta-rap took off, you were again listening to Tribe's *The Low End Theory*. And in 1993, when G-funk was being hailed as the new sound of rap, you were listening to Tribe's masterpiece *Midnight Marauders*. Tribe accompanied you as you grew up. They were a reappraisal of what rap could talk about. Tribe were the weird-beards of the Native Tongues stable who ended up most clearly transcending and surpassing it.

The members of A Tribe Called Quest were all born in 1970, they were a decade younger than Bambaataa's generation, and it told in the confused and kaleidoscopic aesthetic sensibility of their music. Tribe were probably the first rap crew to absorb jazz not just as a sample source but as a playful mindset. Their sound on that first album was confected from even more bizarre sources than Prince Paul was mining for De La Soul. Crucially, it was the progression you sensed in Tribe's music. *The Low End Theory* changed things entirely, a dubby, jazzy, spacey and spooked sound that suited the light-touch solidity of Phife and Q-Tip's rhymes perfectly. The perfect response to the newly tightened sample-clearance guidelines.

Q-Tip's onward importance as talent-spotter and producer would be vital after Tribe's mid-nineties demise, but what stuck with you was how Tribe spoke to you not as pissed-off teenagers (as so much late eighties rap had) but as doubtful fledgling adults, clinging to youthful freedom, aware that responsibility was knocking at the door. Tribe's music is still one of the most addictive bodies of work in hip hop.

JUNGLE BROTHERS

The Jungle Brothers were the solid foundation of the Native Tongues stable and yet the members flirted openly with the possibilities of leaving hip hop behind altogether. Jungle Bros predated the jazz-rap inflections of A Tribe Called Quest and De La Soul, embraced an Afrocentric perspective, forayed into pure dance music, came back and were rejected for it by both hip-hop and mainstream audiences. The industry frequently were confused by them and didn't know what to do with them.

In giving a sound and a name to the whole Native Tongues movement the Jungle Brothers took their cues from two sources, James Brown and Afrika Bambaataa, the former in terms of their moniker and sound-sources and the latter in terms of genre-hopping glee and wider politics. Like Bambaataa, they'd see their role as fundamentally one of education, uplift and positivity. The Jungle Brothers sought to enhance black life by educating black people about their role in history generally and African culture specifically.

So far so worthy, so potentially dull, but what saved the Jungle Brothers beyond their rhetoric was the slapdash nuttiness of their music. They were among the first crews to pay big dues not just to old funk and soul but to other hip hop and *Straight Out The Jungle* is perhaps their most dizzying slab of homage. Even on that album, though you can hear Jungle Brothers roots on dance-label Idler, 'I'll House You', which united the trio with Todd Terry and created a club smash that pretty much birthed the hip-house phenomenon. 1989's *Done By The Forces Of Nature* was easily as good as *3 Feet High* but was sabotaged by Warner Bros's inept treatment and mismarketing of the group. If you stuck around for the fantastic *Raw Deluxe* in 1996 you were reminded of just how frustrating Warner's confusion about the Jungle Brothers really was. No excuses now not to dig out and enjoy all three albums immediately.

BLACK SHEEP

If any group are in danger of falling through the cracks of any re-telling of the Native Tongues story then it's Black Sheep, whose *A Wolf In Sheep's Clothing* was perhaps the most startling record the stable gave us. Where their comrades could come across as furrow-browed, preachy, sometimes a little too correct for their own good, there was nothing correct about Black Sheep. They came across as pranksters, comedians, belligerent bastards, calculatedly offensive if they wanted to be, always with a vision they wanted to engulf you with.

Andres 'Dres' Titus and William 'Mista Lawnge' Mcclean met in North Carolina in 1983. One night, Lawnge was sharing a club bill with Sparkie Dee when Dee's DJ, Red Alert, told him that if he ever made it to the Big Apple, he should give him a call. Lawnge did just that in 1985, hooking up with the Jungle Brothers and A Tribe Called Quest before calling Titus in to form Black Sheep. There's a hint throughout *A Wolf In Sheep's Clothing* that, although partly impressed by the Afrocentric consciousness of their peers, the Sheep couldn't help maintaining an out-of-towners amusement at the po-facedness of their allies. Tracks like 'Black With NV (No Vision)' and 'To Whom It May Concern' harshly criticised upwardly mobile black yuppies while 'Butt... In The Meantime' and the unforgettable 'Strobelite Honey' took a piss-taking attitude toward sexist hip-hop archetypes that was pitched perfectly between homage and heresy. It was a textural riot of spoken word, strange accents,

knockabout, skit-heavy slapstick and splattergun pop
reinvention, Black Sheep music instantly recalls the
heady, giddy, pre-sample-clearance peak of avant-garde
NYC rap.

KOOL DJ RED ALERT

The Native Tongues movement in hip-hop wasn't quite
a crew, or a posse, or anything that had been seen in
hip hop previously. It was perhaps the last time that
hip hop attempted a wholesale change of direction,
a recalibration based not on the usual affiliations of
geography or along political and cultural lines that
brought like minds together. Crucial to the Native
Tongues movement was the influence of Bambaataa's
Zulu Nation, but the Native Tongues shed the quasi-
religious overtones of Bam's congregation, kept the
Afrocentrism and cultural awareness and rendered it
altogether sunnier, cosier, happier.

The core of the Native Tongues were brought
together by Bambaataa's own Kool DJ Red Alert, who
recruited many of the Native Tongues stable, including
A Tribe Called Quest and Monie Love to his Red Alert
management roster. He also helped out when the
Jungle Brothers's label Warlock utterly mismanaged
the release of their debut LP, salvaging 'I'll House You',
putting it out on the Idler imprint, and turning it into the
first hip-house hit to come from outside of Chicago.
Tommy Boy Records, who'd brought out Bambaataa's
Planet Rock, picked up on De La Soul and fellow Native
Tongue, Queen Latifah. The loosely agglomerated Native
Tongues movement also pulled in Brand Nubian (banned
from further mention in this book thanks to their vile
homophobia), Busta Rhymes fledgling crew Leaders of
the New School, Black Sheep, Chi-Ali and the Beatnuts,
but at no point did you feel that this was a confined
dictatorial 'crew' as such. Rather, Native Tongues music
seemed to be recorded in a different headspace to any
hip hop that had occurred before it. Loose, jazzy, the

sound of sleepovers as Phife Dawg would have it – there
was a sense of experimentation but crucially no sense
at all that any member of the collective wanted to outdo
anyone, either each other or the rest of hip hop.

In contrast to hip hop's bull-pit competitiveness,
Native Tongues music seemed to grow from
collaboration and wide-eyed adolescence. That
gentleness, that sense of teenage exploration and
relaxed, faintly stoned noodling, would have the greatest
impact on hip hop. Conscious rappers and artists like
Common, the Roots, Erykah Badu, Slum Village, J Dilla,
Mos Def, Talib Kweli all owe Native Tongues a debt.
As they grew up, the music of these artists frequently
outgrew the Native Tongues remit but the movement
Red Alert started had a lasting impact on all thoughtful,
unclichéd rap since.

PRINCE PAUL

The genius behind De La Soul's emergence cut his teeth
and learned his trade as part of Stetsasonic, one of the
great forgotten crews of eighties rap. Stetsasonic were
one of the first hip-hop crews to use a live band and
unlike many eighties rap groups always maintained a
profoundly positive and articulate mindset in their music.
Stetsasonic honed their live production by going on tour
with Public Enemy, LL Cool J, Whodini, Eric B and Rakim,
EPMD and Run-DMC, but while their albums such as *In
Full Gear* got plaudits, they got few sales.

It was production that really fired Paul's imagination,
in particular Hank Shocklee's Bomb Squad productions
for Public Enemy that were at the time blowing hip-hop
fans' minds with their multi-layered, densely textured,
sample-heavy complexity. Paul's genius was in applying
the Bomb Squad's openness of technique to a totally
new vault of sources, records no one else was sampling,
diverting from the normal funk and soul roots of hip-hop
production to incorporate sixties pop, seventies soft-
rock, weird spoken-word records and folk records from

the pre-pop age, soundtracks, language-instruction albums, anything that he felt could be strip-mined for valuable material. Listen to *3 Feet High*, or even better, the work he did with 3rd Bass on their fantastic *The Cactus Album* and what you hear is all this junk marshalled with an exquisite finesse. Paul's sound, often uniquely in rap using deliberately vintage equipment, was inimitable and much in demand by everyone from the Native Tongues across to harder-core artists like BDP and Big Daddy Kane. His work after his break with De La Soul, including the incredible collaboration with fellow ex-Stetsasonic member Frukwan on the RZA-curated supergroup Gravediggaz and with Dan the Automator in Handsome Boy Modeling School, shouldn't be underestimated either. Prince Paul was the ultimate post-Bomb Squad, pre-sample-clearance producer.

Column 11

45 De **89** — De La Soul		
46 Tq **89** — A Tribe Called Quest	**51** Gs **91** — Gang Starr	**56** Tu **91** — Tupac
47 Ju **88** — Jungle Brothers	**52** P **92** — Pharcyde	**57** Sd **93** — Snoop Dogg
48 Bl **91** — Black Sheep	**53** Ms **91** — Main Source	**58** Ic **90** — Ice Cube
49 Kd **86** — Kool DJ Red Alert	**54** Km **91** — KMD	**59** Wc **95** — WC and the Maad Circle
50 Pp **89** — Prince Paul	**55** Dp **89** — DJ Premier	**60** Sk **91** — Suge Knight
		61 Wg **94** — Warren G

GANG STARR

Soon after De La Soul's success, and inspired in part by the Native Tongues's use of jazz loops and breaks, a whole welter of deep-crate diggers and thoughtful MCs sprang up, an anti-movement of whom Gang Starr were leading lights. Their second and third albums, *Step In The Arena* and *Daily Operation*, are their touchstone releases, although there's gold to be found on all of their output bar their somewhat clumsy debut.

Step In The Arena is the final word in the conversation started by A Tribe Called Quest's *The Low End Theory*. It's the perfect absorption of jazz into rap, while *Daily Operation* is a straight-up twisted out hardcore masterpiece. On both, the match between DJ Premier and Guru the MC is perfect. Each balancing the other; Premier with his uniquely insistent loops and beats, his twisted meld of the two, and Guru with his uniquely thoughtful raps, sometimes forced and ungainly but always absolutely fitting the maelstrom like a glove. Gang Starr managed to make music that was instantly understandable and enjoyable but that revealed depths the more you listened. It was music with total integrity but none of the over-earnestness that implies. Guru imposed a kind of awed agitation on the listener like no one since Rakim, the instant need to learn every line, lines that stay with you and sustain you. Gang Starr are the essential component of any true hip-hop fans collection and still the gold standard for any hip-hop duo starting out.

PHARCYDE

The Pharcyde didn't meet on the street or in record stores. They were dancers who met on the late eighties underground club circuit in LA, even serving a stint on the Fox series *In Living Color*.

MCs and producers Tre Slimkid3 Hardson, Imani Wilcox and Romye Robinson hooked up with Derrick

Stewart in 1990. Under the tutelage of Reggie Andrews, a local high-school music teacher, the group learned about the music industry and recording before getting a deal with Delicious Vinyl in 1991 and unleashing their stunning debut *Bizarre Ride II The Pharcyde* a year later. Live, they were as fast-moving as their music, and you can hear something of the terpsichorean throughout that debut. Everything was danceable, made for movement, kinetic. *Bizarre Ride* was one of the great early nineties West Coast rap LPs for those looking for an alternative to the suffocating insularity and strictures of gangsta. The Pharcyde jitterbugged past the more reverent modal stylings of A Tribe Called Quest and Gang Starr, resurrecting the full lurid frenetics of a Cab Calloway or Count Basie, insisting that LA could just as easily draw on its psychedelic and showbiz roots as document the same gritty streets over and over again. This was an alternate route most of their West Coast contemporaries ignored but one that means the Pharcyde, unlike those contemporaries, will be returned to with fondness and danced to again with new steps. If you dance to N.W. Frickin A., you're gonna look stupid, I guarantee it.

MAIN SOURCE

One of the hidden gems of hip-hop history, a band who only really came together on one album and then went their separate ways, but in the process created a classic that's deeply beloved by hip-hop fans of the Golden Age. People won't part with Main Source's *Breaking Atoms*, they won't lend it you and seem almost reticent to make a tape or a copy of such a holy document. If you're lucky enough to find a copy, it'll probably be scratched to buggery but you should still play it, and play it with great fondness because it's a corker.

Like so many classic albums of this era, *Breaking Atoms* has to be careful what it pulls from. It creates sumptuously funky music from sources no one could trace using a Synclavier and an SP-1200. Ignoring the

P-funk and James Brown samples the rest of rap was busy running dry, Main Source's production team of Large Professor, DJ K-Cut and Sir Scratch culled their collages from records you couldn't imagine and made one of the most effective, smoked-out, sampladelic masterpieces that rap had ever produced.

This musical breadth was matched with some incredibly clever wordplay. Check out the baseball-themed, police-brutality banger 'Just A Friendly Game Of Baseball' and the heartbreakingly dysfunctional 'Looking At The Front Door' for rappers bringing wit and restraint to difficult subjects. Large Pro and K would go on to mould so much future hip hop and here they also give Akinyele and Nas their debut cameos on the stunning 'Live At The Barbecue'.

After *Breaking Atoms*, Large Pro would make several more classics, but nothing touches the work he accomplished with Main Source. The first rolling out of a hip-hop legend and a still-dizzying highlight of rap's most creative age. A gem.

KMD

Every hip-hop fan likes having an album they think is crazy-underrated, unfairly ignored, an album they like getting evangelical about. For me it's KMD's *Mr Hood*, a record whose absence in any hip-hop fan's collection sends me into fits of exaggerated disgust. For many, by the time it'd come out, *Mr Hood* was simply an adjunct to the 'daisy-age' story but I'd call it one of the greatest lost works of American art in the twentieth century. KMD were perhaps the unluckiest genii rap ever gave us. MC Serch of 3rd Bass discovered MC Zevlove X (who'd later re-emerge as MF Doom), DJ Subroc and Onyx the Birthstone Kid and made them a key element in 3rd Bass's RIF Productions roster. *Mr Hood*, their debut, slipped out in late 1991 on Elektra and bewitched anyone who heard it.

From the sleeve to the music within, *Mr Hood* was a detonation of stereotypes from the off. Letting their wit and sense of wonder push through both political correctness and conservative revisionism, KMD shone a bright light through the burning issues of 1991, interrogated rap, stereotypes, race, sexism, politics, prejudice and hope with a crackpot wit and a whacked-out spirit unmatched by anyone else. None of which would've made *Mr Hood* so potent if the music hadn't been so instantaneously dazzling. *Mr Hood* took Prince Paul's cartoon lunacy and calmed it down, focused it into a series of skits and tracks that flowed brilliantly, each three minutes a little pocket universe of its own, each track populated by at least a dozen moments of hand-to-mouth, gasp-worthy wonder you'd have to hit rewind on. The threadbare concept of the happenings in a barbershop and KMD's increasingly fractious meetings with the straight talking Mr Hood of the title attain the feel of a growing revelation. It's a masterpiece.

The follow up LP, *Black Bastards*, was destroyed by Elektra over its controversial cover art (a lynched 'sambo' cartoon) and KMD's treatment by the music business after the death of DJ Subroc (they were dropped by Elektra the same week) is of lasting shame to hip hop. Remedy this by getting *Mr Hood*, an essential.

DJ PREMIER

You get the feeling with Premo, as you did with the Bomb Squad and Prince Paul, that here is someone who sees sound before they hear it, or can even attempt to sculpt it into reality. DJ Premier's music transforms the sonic chiaroscuros and smears of colour that music abstractly paints in his mind into a living breathing funky reality. He's the solidification of how the selector-role returned to DJing in the 1990s. He had the ability to dig the right crate for the right records, to find loops no one else could, secure sounds otherwise lost and brutalise them, make them snap to a different beat. Frequently those beats are chopped, sliced, diced and re-rendered in arrhythmic waves, refusing to release you, refusing to make sense. Listen to Gang Starr's 'Soliloquy Of Chaos', 'Beyond Comprehension' or 'Too Deep'. Listen to Jeru the Damaja's 'Come Clean'. Frequently the collage of sound on top of the beat similarly refuses to behave itself, refracts down the drain, seeps up to space. Listen to Gang Starr's 'Take It Personal' or Group Home's 'Livin' Proof' or Jeru's 'D.Original' (indeed anything off Jeru's *Sun Rises In The East* and *Wrath Of The Math* sets). There are, sometimes, sounds that are plain gorgeous, sounds that break your heart with the repetitive wonder of them, the glows of smoky, gritty joy they contain. Listen to Crooklyn Dodgers's *Return Of The Crooklyn Dodgers* or Gang Starr's 'Code Of The Streets' and tell me Premo shouldn't be considered as one of those producers who gave us some of music's highest points of beauty in the nineties, moments from where the rest of music looked awfully graceless and guileless. He may be a one-trick pony, sure, but it was an amazing trick.

Column 12

		62 94 **Na** Nas
51 91 **Gs** Gang Starr	56 91 **Tu** Tupac	63 94 **Bs** Biggie Smalls
52 92 **P** Pharcyde	57 93 **Sd** Snoop Dogg	64 93 **Md** Mobb Deep
53 91 **Ms** Main Source	58 90 **Ic** Ice Cube	65 93 **Bm** Black Moon
54 91 **Km** KMD	59 95 **Wc** WC and the Maad Circle	66 97 **Se** Sean Combs
55 89 **Dp** DJ Premier	60 91 **Sk** Suge Knight	67 92 **Pr** Pete Rock
	61 94 **Wg** Warren G	

TUPAC

The Golden Age so often yearned for now was so often not golden. Pity poor Tupac, the most comprehensively misunderstood and overrated rapper in hip-hop history. His martyrdom made him, and distorts him. His death turned his crimes (fights that killed six-year-old bystanders, sexual assault) into forgivable, life scars that made those dreamboat eyes more poignant. The conspiracy theories since his death bubble endlessly on (latest you heard, he was never shot and is living under the Giza pyramids, working on new tracks in collaboration with Jay-Z and our other Illuminati lizard overlords).

All the conjecture, all the blank dumb hymn-book re-assertions of his 'legendary' status, blind many to the fact that the vast bulk of Tupac's recorded work doesn't really warrant revisiting. Harsh, perhaps, to call him an actor who didn't particularly care about rap (which of course made Death Row his perfect home), but the fatal thing for Pac was that he rarely exerted even the remotest quality control over his music, and was too profligate with what talent he had. So while we have a lot of work to pick over, proportionally little of it remains memorable. He made too much middling music. More damagingly, the coastal turf-wars that Tupac was all-too happy to perpetuate were perhaps the most boring and bewildering aspect of hip hop in the nineties, setting a pattern of pointless beef that hip hop's adhered to ever since. His posthumous canonisation may well have been good for business. It's uncontroversial now to say that his sainthood shouldn't obscure his weaknesses.

SNOOP DOGG

You heard about Snoop before you heard him for real. His contributions to Dre's 'Deep Cover' and 'Nuthin But A G Thang' ensured that the advance orders for *Doggystyle* were immense, and made it a hit before it even came out. These orders were procured in the time between Calvin 'Snoop' Broadus getting out of jail and the moment after the 1993 MTV Awards when he surrendered himself to police custody to face drive-by murder charges. The lurid details of Snoop's life boosted his profile undoubtedly. Before *Doggystyle* hit you knew he'd given a tape to pal Warren G who'd passed it to his step-bro Dr Dre who'd then used Snoop on *The Chronic* to great effect. *Doggystyle* lived up to its own hype by being almost a carbon-copy of *The Chronic*, a smart move, and featuring some gloriously gratuitously offensive rhymes (ghostwritten by that sick twist Too Short) over some of Dre's most eargasmically sumptuous arrangements.

Crucial to Snoop's lasting success is his truly unique character, his irresistible charm, the warmth and natural good humour. Slight, lanky, gangling, fey – his speech and rapping voice were so mellow they seemed to emerge from the red-eyed daze of a perma-stoned rude-boy. His self-aware slackerdom, his sense of shooting the breeze and talking a good game, made those moments when he did issue threats all the more menacing. His departure from Death Row was a smart move, and he's been making smart moves ever since, culminating in the genre-changing 'Drop It Like It's Hot' and his collaborations with Dâm-Funk in the last decade. He is a survivor and one of the most inimitable voices in rap. From the kindling that is much West Coast gangsta music, this is gold worth salvaging.

ICE CUBE

58 · 90

Ic

Ice Cube

Amazing how much better Cube got when he turned his back on his past and struck out for the East. South Central born 'n' bred, he'd been rapping since the early eighties, working with Dre and the World Class Wreckin' Cru since 1985. As writer and spitter of the best and most politically suggestive verses on *Straight Outta Compton*, Cube left N.W.A. in disgust at the contract terms Jerry Heller and Ruthless were offering him, signed for Priority and proceeded to make three of the best solo rap albums of all time. His single 'AmeriKKKa's Most Wanted' in the 1990s united him with the Bomb Squad whom he so admired, and was an unforgettable blast of righteous ire and fury. In 1992, his three-million selling *The Predator* released in the wake of the LA riots, is seen by most as his masterpiece, a beautifully crafted mix of the elegiac (the unforgettable 'It Was A Good Day'), polemical and paranoiac ('When Will They Shoot?') that debuted at No. 1 in both the pop and rap charts, the first album in history to do so. For this writer though his high point is *Death Certificate*, a loosely woven concept album about life and death that contains both his most wonderfully offensive lyrics and his most scintillating music. If you're white, Jewish, a woman or in any way a decent human being you will be offended by *Death Certificate* but if you have two brain cells to rub together you'll also massively enjoy it as a diagnosis of black and white America that remains unparalleled. Cube's later career is best forgot as a rash of bandwagon-jumping mistakes but for nearly five years he was absolutely central to rap and a cherishably furious presence in hip hop.

WC AND THE MAAD CIRCLE

Who? Well, precisely. I cannot let any analysis of West Coast hip hop go by without talking about the great artists unjustly forgotten. There was so much going on in California that wasn't G-funk, that wasn't Ruthless or Death Row-affiliated, that didn't just make P-funk into pop. Kinfolk's incredible *Each And Every Day*, from Oakland the wonderful Souls Of Mischief and political firebrand Paris's re-appropriation of G-funk as *Guerrilla Funk* for revolutionary ends, Compton's King Tee's massively influential late eighties drunk-hop, the Coup's amazing body of work (especially the astonishing *Pick A Bigger Weapon*) and, perhaps most forgotten of all, WC and the Maad Circle's stupendous *Curb Servin'*. Ring any bells? Thought not. It should.

There was nothing inherently wrong with G-funk or the idea of California rappers talking about gangs and criminality. *Curb Servin'* stirs the same sound-stew of P-funk and synthetic influences as Dre and Warren G were stirring. But my God, it does it so much more effectively, puts it on tracks that crucially don't have the over-deodorised cleanliness and correctness of Dre and Warren G's productions. These tracks are sexy, excessive, thumping, impolite, and the life that WC raps about feels realer than the supra-cool loftiness of so much gangsta-rap. The gang life, the gangsta life, is here portrayed as offering complete security and endless hassle, a fatalist routine of day-to-day criminality shot through with moments of reflection and rage, the mind-lint that accumulates on a stake-out, waiting for your dealer, standing on a corner, stepping home at dawn. As a snapshot of a time and place it's more accurate than anything Death Row or Ruthless gave us and shouldn't be ignored in any analysis of West Coast rap, although it nearly always is. The official story, especially with hip hop, so often doesn't give you the whole story.

SUGE KNIGHT

Whether repeatedly violently assaulting women, dangling Vanilla Ice off a balcony by his ankles, sending thugs round to intimidate label bosses, managers and artists, attacking random underlings and journalists, torturing and robbing promoters, fleeing the scene of fatal accidents, provoking rivals into pointless bouts of turf-warfare that ended up hurting everyone but him, setting up shootings and assassinations (allegedly), or running Death Row Records like a money-laundering gulag, there's no doubt that Suge Knight was quick-tempered, hot-headed and nasty. In taking Dre from Ruthless and enabling him to create *The Chronic* and *Doggystyle*, his place in the growth of West Coast hip hop is crucial. At its peak, Death Row sold more than 18 million albums in four years, earning more than $325 million. It gave former-jock

Suge Knight a rich and infamous lifestyle, in which he basked. This was, financially, unheard-of territory for hip hop but you wonder, confronted with the sheer amount of felonious behaviour that Knight engaged in, whether there wasn't something deeply institutionalised about the man, something that made him more comfortable behind bars. At no point in his career does it ever occur to Knight to 'keep his head down', let things blow over. He craves the spotlight more than his artists, repeatedly gets involved in monumentally stupid acts of sadism and cruelty almost guaranteed to keep him in court or in jail. Speculation about his involvement in the killings of Tupac and Biggie Smalls has always been rife but what's perhaps most apparent about Knight is his willing exploitation of that speculation, his love of revelling in all that no-smoke-without-fire intrigue. Tellingly, artists and DJs started to leave Death Row in droves very early in that label's history, because the smart criminals are the ones you've never heard of. Knight is perhaps hip hop's first real criminal-as-mogul. There've been many who've tried to claim the same ever since.

WARREN G

The man who perfected the West Coast production style that'd become known as G-funk.

All hip-hop production of the early nineties had to find ways round the sample-clearance strictures the Biz Markie case had thrown up. For East Coast producers it was about making the thieving less obvious, finding untraceable samples and then further erasing the evidence-trail via studio manipulation. For the West Coast, land of plastic surgery and porn, it was about synthetics, multi-layered synthesisers, slow grooves that suited the sun-struck streets and the jeeps, fleshing things out with backing vocals and conventionally melodic choruses, pillaging P-funk for loops, slapping on a high-pitched portmanteau saw-wave synth lead. With all that in place, G-funk happened. It used way fewer samples, filled out details with live instrumentation and made rap behave itself, made rap follow the narrative structures and harmonic progressions of mainstream pop.

The Mobb music scene of the Bay Area had prefigured G-funk a little, Oakland's Too Short was a heavy influence (his laconic drawling rapping style was definitely noticed by Snoop), but it was G-funk that broke through via Dre's *The Chronic* and hits like Warren G's 'Regulate'. It'd find its way into records by Above the Law, Tupac, Nate Dogg, Spice 1 and damn-near everyone working in West Coast rap in the early nineties. Beyond *Doggystyle*, *The Chronic* and G's *The G-Funk Era*, no one listens to those records anymore. They were mainly terrible.

Column 13

		62 94 **Na** Nas	68 91 **Ch** Cypress Hill
	56 91 **Tu** Tupac	63 94 **Bs** Biggie Smalls	69 94 **Di** D.I.T.C.
	57 93 **Sd** Snoop Dogg	64 93 **Md** Mobb Deep	70 93 **Ak** Alkaholiks
	58 90 **Ic** Ice Cube	65 93 **Bm** Black Moon	71 92 **R** Redman
	59 95 **Wc** WC and the Maad Circle	66 97 **Se** Sean Combs	72 92 **St** Steve Rifkind
	60 91 **Sk** Suge Knight	67 92 **Pr** Pete Rock	73 93 **B** Beatnuts
	61 94 **Wg** Warren G		

NAS

The first time you heard Nas was on Main Source's 'Live At The Barbecue' and you knew you were witness to the first outing of someone special. By the time Nas was releasing his debut *Illmatic* in 1994, and you were hearing tracks like 'Halftime' and 'NY State Of Mind', you knew you were hearing one of the greatest *ever*. Born Nasir Jones, son of jazz musician Olu Dara, Nas had dropped out of high-school in the eighth grade, seeking his own education on the streets of the Queensbridge projects and in literature. Both informed his future ability to crush street-smart imagery with finely honed wordplay. *Illmatic*, produced by the cream of NYC production talent (Pete Rock, Premier, Large Pro), was one of rap's finest ever debuts, a shuffling maze of beats and rhymes that felt like a stumbling voyage around the same streets Nas stalked. It never felt like cultural tourism, rather *Illmatic* felt like a tour around Jones's physical environment and also the internal mental impact of that environment, his supra-aware consciousness, the poetic flights and very human doubt that dwelled within. Nas would create great music after *Illmatic*, but his debut still captures his art before it made any concessions to pop, before his needless beefs with Jay-Z, at a sublime moment when his talent was focused on the truth and not the smoke and mirrors of status. East Coast, mid-nineties hip hop perfected.

BIGGIE SMALLS

A big, soft, mommy's boy at heart, a middle-class dealer in package-trip ghetto chicanery who'd only passed up Mum's apple pie for an opportunity to sell crack to those poorer and less fortunate than himself. We're told frequently that when Biggie joined Sean 'Puffy' Combs in moving from Uptown to form Bad Boy it was an 'epochal' moment. I can't see it myself, as it led to so much middling music. *Ready To Die* is far from the classic of its romantic reputation and like much of Biggie's work it's patchy. Brilliant when it does hit ('Big Poppa') but the gold is surrounded by so much shit you need tongs and a clothes-peg on your nose to pluck it out.

The tragic early passing of Smalls cuts a bit harder than Tupac's death. You do feel that, given time, pushed by the right producers, he might have eventually created something great, or been a part of something great. What Biggie had in his favour was his voice. When he flowed he flowed smooth, but the lyrics he penned were too frequently lazy rehashes and braggadocio coasting, so you never really got the sense that he was pushing himself, or that anyone around him would have the *cojones* to suggest he should expand or complicate his simplistic schemata and methods. Like Tupac, anyone calling him a rap god or the greatest of all time immediately reveals themselves as someone who doesn't know rap music. Quite how someone can be the greatest ever when they only released one album while alive is beyond me. Don't let the felling of either of hip hop's supposed twin towers fool you. Tragic losses both, but not to hip hop.

MOBB DEEP

Mobb Deep were first heard, for a lot of us, on the radio. Hip-hop radio is commonplace now, or rather, hip hop has so infected mainstream radio playlists that specialist shows and networks increasingly seem like relics from a more segregated age. But Tim Westwood's shows were of massive significance to hip-hop devotees in the UK and the show that performed the same feat over in the States was undoubtedly the *Stretch Armstrong and Bobbito Show*. It broadcast on Columbia University's WKCR network for four hours every early Thursday morning from 1990 to 1998 and was picked up by Hot 97 from 1996 to 1998. Like the UK magazine *Hip Hop Connection* (undoubtedly the best rap magazine ever), the best ever hip-hop radio show was by fans, for fans. They'd play vinyl, demo tapes, ADAT reels and featured exclusives that

no other hip-hop radio network could match. There were
live freestyles and appearances by names that would turn
out to be some of the biggest in rap. Reading the roll-call
and track listings now reads simultaneously like a who's
who of the nineties and a prophesy of the next decade's
biggest names too. As the first show to play the likes of
Biggie, O.C., Jay-Z, Nas, Eminem, Mobb Deep, D.I.T.C.,
Wu-Tang Clan and Busta Rhymes, the duo's shows would
be taped, then jammed in Walkmans and beat-boxes for
the week afterwards, just as Westwood's were in the UK.
If you can find bootlegs, get 'em. They still sound fresh
and for both artists and fans, they remain both a gateway
into some of the greatest hip-hop music of all time and a
definitive index of the vitality, strength and diversity of hip
hop's Golden Age.

Prior to *The Infamous*, one of the greatest hardcore
hip-hop albums of all time, Mobb Deep were only of
interest to hip-hop heads because of their collaborators.
Straight out of Queensbridge, New York, an area that also
gave us Marley Marl and Nas, MD's Havoc and Prodigy
recorded their debut LP *Juvenile Hell* as teenagers,
with Premo and Large Pro at the controls. Havoc also
guested on Black Moon's 'U Da Man' but *The Infamous*
was something else altogether. Self-produced bar a
few final mix-downs by the Abstract (Q-Tip's producer
pseudonym), it was the perfect combination of mid-
nineties NYC dead-on lyrics and music that hit on a
sublime mix of scary, scratchy stereo-strafed samples
and punishing, icy beats. Like Nas (who guested) Mobb's
lyrics were simultaneously locked in on their own world
and touched with presentiments of wider afflictions,
mortality, and fate. A grim yet gorgeous record wherein
doomy fatalistic words and themes recurred like totems
of safety. Tracks like 'Survival Of The Fittest' and 'Shook
Ones' were some of the most chilling, atmospheric hip
hop of the decade, haunted by ghosts of melody yet
always skewered by brutally hard-hitting beats, a style
of beat-making and lyrical connection with real street

terrors that no one else could match. Greater fame would come MD's way (its follow up *Hell On Earth* is about three-quarters as good which still makes it awesome) but *The Infamous* remains one of nineties hip hop's most enduringly shocking, eternally beautiful moments.

BLACK MOON

What was happening in the early-to-mid-nineties in hip hop curiously mirrored what was happening in rock 'n' roll. Just as grunge proved the perfect antidote to LA poodle-rock, an introverted and alternative arrived for b-boys in the mid-nineties who were finding the moneyed-up triumphalism of gangsta-rap was no longer telling their story. We wanted music that reflected our lives, and those lives were in the main fairly miserable, fairly dark, fairly fucked up. The focus of hip hop moved from one of mass appeal to the basements and bedrooms and headphones, the bleak company of yourself.

Black Moon were among the first to chart that inward shift, the welter of doomy psychedelic hip hop that defined the mid-nineties and laid the template for the re-emergence of underground rap at the end of the decade. From the off they weren't interested in signing to a major label or losing any control of their destiny. Setting up their own production (Da Beatminerz) and management (Duck Down) companies endeared them to rap's elder strugglers. KRS-One called their debut, *Enta Da Stage*, the 'phattest shit I've heard in a long time'. It's a stone-cold masterpiece of rap, a new kind of aggression as much about what's not said as what's said, menace simmering in the silences, and massively influential on the East Coast. Musically, the Beatminerz cooked up beats and bass-loops so subterranean they seemed belched up from the pits of hell, so that every flickering detail of the treble walks a tightrope over this lo-end abyss. This was as close as hip hop ever got to dub. Black Moon created a sound that still engrosses hip-hop listeners two decades later.

SEAN COMBS

In 1991, when Harlemite business-major dropout Sean Combs threw parties while interning at NYC's Uptown Records, an AIDS-benefit he threw with Heavy D was oversold massively. The resultant crush and stampede at the CCNY Gym resulted in nine people being killed. Combs moved on. In the mid-nineties, when his label Bad Boy had benefited from their biggest signing, Biggie, going multi-platinum on *Ready To Die*, he and others at Bad Boy fostered and fed a growing, visible feud with Tupac Shakur, Suge Knight and Death Row records that possibly resulted in the deaths of Shakur and Smalls. Releasing *Life After Death* 16 days after Biggie's death, the album ended up selling 10 million copies and became one of the biggest-selling rap albums of all time. A couple of months later he released his own solo debut, *No Way Out*. His tribute to Biggie, 'I'll Be Missing You', was included, as were four other terrible singles and several other watered-down and commercialised songs. The album won Grammys, sold millions, and made him one of the most powerful people in hip hop. Combs changed his name from Puff Daddy to P Diddy to plain Diddy with the rebranding agility of any multinational. He rapidly started diversifying: restaurants, clothing lines, perfume, TV networks, in an omnivorous way that was massively influential on future Svengalis like Jay-Z and Master P. He's currently worth about $700 million. It's arguable whether his legacy is simply one of wealth creation. His influence on music has been almost all bad.

PETE ROCK

There's a warm narcotic buzz that creeps down your body, from scalp to toe (with particularly delicious massaging effects on your shoulders) when you think about Pete Rock's triple-shot of wonder that started with *Mecca And The Soul Brother* in 1992, continued through *The Main Ingredient*, released in 1994, and wound up with

Soul Survivor in 1998. These were touchstone recordings for an unashamed new trend in hip-hop listening; they were albums you heard at home with a big spliff on the go. Sacred tablets for headphone-hebephrenics everywhere, music that took jazz and funk and dub and tapped their spiritual depths as much as their sonic detail. Bad jazz-rap wore jazz like an armband; Pete Rock re-invoked it.

Pete Rock's mentor was Marley Marl, one of only a few producers who could match PR for consistent, instinctive studio magic. With Premo and Large Pro nipping at his heels, it's surprising what a relaxed, nothing-to-prove and effortlessly great feel Pete Rock creates on his productions. Through the nineties he worked with pretty much everyone in hip hop and always created unforgettable backdrops for some of the greatest tracks in rap. He was the producer's producer.

Column 14

62 94 **Na** Nas	**68** 91 **Ch** Cypress Hill	
63 94 **Bs** Biggie Smalls	**69** 94 **Di** D.I.T.C.	**74** 93 **Wu** Wu-Tang Clan
64 93 **Md** Mobb Deep	**70** 93 **Ak** Alkaholiks	**75** 95 **Ra** Raekwon
65 93 **Bm** Black Moon	**71** 92 **R** Redman	**76** 95 **Gz** GZA
66 97 **Se** Sean Combs	**72** 92 **St** Steve Rifkind	**77** 96 **Rl** Real Live
67 92 **Pr** Pete Rock	**73** 93 **B** Beatnuts	**78** 93 **Rz** RZA

CYPRESS HILL

The debut self-titled LP was only available on import, a holy chalice of amazing beats and an addictive Mexicano/Cubano delivery. The critical consensus around Cypress Hill was that they were using East Coast techniques of rhyme invention and applying them to West Coast living, albeit a stoner's view of LA life. In truth they were reconfiguring hip-hop syntax around their own Latino roots, letting in new vocab and speaking this weird, new hybrid pidgin-gangsta in voices quite unlike anything else in hip hop. The whiny delinquent tones of Louis Freese (B-Real) and Sen Reyes (Sen Dog) gained authority because they sounded real, like you were walking down a barrio street hearing this lurid backchat popping out of every passing window, every front stoop.

Cypress Hill made weed sound less like a habit and more like a way of life, an altered reality, a different perspective. Behind this, Muggs's productions were unmistakable, had the contact high addictiveness of chicken crank, a heat-stricken acid-fried sound that seemed to stalk streets off the beaten path, stumbling into neighbourhoods united not just by race but by poverty and the crushing need for hedonistic escape. For three albums, *Cypress Hill*, *Black Sunday* and *Temples Of Boom*, Cypress Hill were the wake-and-bake rap of choice for any self-respecting toker psychonaut. Still sounding as ill as ever.

D.I.T.C.

This side of the Wu-Tang, and after the Juice Crew, the Diggin' In The Crates posse were probably the most important set of rappers, DJs and producers New York City gave us in the nineties, many of whom created that decade's finest hip-hop music. Most of the crew had been involved in hip hop since the mid-eighties but the D.I.T.C. moniker gave them a home and a focus and a feeling of shared wisdom and power. Diamond D, Lord

Finesse, Buckwild and Showbiz were the production talent, genius crate-diggers responsible for some of the greatest beats and arrangements in nineties rap.

To understand why they so perfectly sum up Nuyorican hip-hop sensibilities, that love of banging production and mentally incisive rhymes, check out D and the Psychotic Neurotic's masterly *Stunts, Blunts and Hip Hop*, Finesse's *Funky Technician* and *Awakening* sets, Buck's work with the magnificent O.C. on the mind-blowing *Word... Life*, Showbiz and A.G.'s incredible *Runaway Slave* and *Goodfellas* albums.

D.I.T.C.'s weakest work came from their most public face: Fat Joe, an artist, who like the similarly globulous Big Pun was big on reputation (and fond of chimichangas) but never exerted enough quality control to deserve the legendary status he's been afforded. Check out Big L's albums instead.

D.I.T.C. are state-of-the-art East Coast hip hop in the mid-nineties. For some of us the greatest sound ever.

ALKAHOLIKS

When hip hop mentions alcohol, which is often, it's usually presented as something to numb pain or live the high-life with, whether it's juvenile thug-rap's love of cheapskate 40oz malt liquor, or gangsta-rap's fetishisation of Cristal, Moët and Hennessy. Alkaholiks talked about drinking in a different way, from a knowledge forged in love, thirst and that delicious way your first hit of the morning massages your shoulders, shades the sun, springs your step. Alkaholiks didn't ever seem overly proud of their predilections but they were hilariously honest about them, populating their music with belches and asides and rushes to the toilet bowl that were alarmingly accurate. No boasting, Alkaholiks talked about the kind of steady, heavy, day-to-day booziness that hip-hop listeners could readily identify with.

Alkaholiks came busting out the unlikely environs of Ohio. J-Ro, Swift and Tash swam into the already well-oiled universe of party-down legend King Tee who was at the time looking for a backing crew. Helping him with his *Triflin'* album, the crew were christened by Tee and following support slots with Ice Cube and KRS-One, signed to Loud who brought out their *21 And Over* and *Coast II Coast* sets which remain perhaps the most luridly, accurately detailed slacker-hop albums ever created. With Alkaholiks and Cypress Hill ruling the roost it's no surprise that a lot of hip-hop fans in the mid-nineties emerged from it all a little off-kilter, often with eyes that pointed in different directions. It's a strong look.

REDMAN

71   92
R
Redman

Busta Rhymes was probably hip hop's biggest oddball talent in the nineties but he's jettisoned in preference of Redman here because Redman, more than most for me, represents all hip-hop outsiders that have thrived, despite working in a culture that prizes teamwork and group-think. Like fellow eccentric loons ODB, Chino XL and New Kingdom, Redman's work was heavily influenced by a prodigious drug intake. Not fast, self-improving, business-minded drugs like Russell Simmons hoovered up but provincial, deranging, slow-building, long-lasting powerful hallucinogens that twist you out of shape for life. Acid, mushrooms, peyote, DMT (hey, stop drooling): these were undoubtedly what fed into Redman's psyche. When he breathed on you with his unforgettable debut *Whut? Thee Album* you got a contact high that lasted for weeks. He came across like a veteran from the off, a cracked, ravaged, bewildering and bewildered voice. His pinnacle is his second album *Dare Iz A Darkside* and the pinnacle of that opus is the astonishing 'Green Island', the epicentre and mind-melting highlight. A woozy, progressively more engulfing fog of shimmering Hawaiian guitar and stoned-funk containing some of the funniest, most puerile doggerel you've ever heard. A towering, psychedelic moment in hip-hop history from one of the greatest mavericks to ever step to the mic. Pretty soon a crew from Staten Island would make such strangeness the biggest sound in hip hop.

STEVE RIFKIND

72		92
	St	
	Steve Rifkind	

Loud Records was the home of so much great hip hop from the mid-nineties and was the brainchild of Steve Rifkind, son of Jules Rifkind, the creator of Spring Records. Spring was the label that in 1979 beat Sugar Hill Records to the punch by releasing the Fatback Band's *Personality Jock*, the first hip-hop record to ever make it into shops.

Setting up Loud in 1991 Rifkind Jr rapidly made it the home for a fantastic selection of hip-hop artists, including Wu-Tang Clan, Mobb Deep, Alkaholiks, Dead Prez, Xzibit, Big Pun and M.O.P. Just as the Def Jam logo was a seal of quality in the eighties, so Loud's logo was in the nineties. Crucially, it was Rifkind's pioneering innovations in promotion that really had a lasting impact on hip hop. The Street Team promotional model he created was based on the simple principles of word-of-mouth advertising, coupled with a street-level knowledge of the subculture being marketed to. He asserted that a record shouldn't even come out before the label knew what the street thought. Rather than PRs stuck in offices making phone calls, Loud's street-team mirrored the graffiti crews and hype-men of hip hop's birth, flyering, stencilling messages and logos in high-traffic urban areas, coordinating giveaways of promo CDs and posters and T-shirts at events, anything that could build a buzz one step at a time from the ground up. By focusing not on the traditional media routes but on DJs, rappers, promoters and radio producers, Rifkind and Loud were able to make inroads into the hip-hop market that mainstream labels found next to impossible. Labels like Bad Boy, No Limits and Roc-A-Fella would learn fast.

73   93

B

Beatnuts

BEATNUTS

The 'Nuts, based in Latino stronghold Corona in Queens, made their name with production and remix work throughout the early nineties for artists as diverse and divergent as Pete Nice, Naughty By Nature, Da Lench Mob, Cypress Hill and Fat Joe. A trio comprising Psycho Les (scary Beatnut), JuJu (posh Beatnut) and Fashion (scary Beatnut again), they'd developed their brilliant Latinate-inflected sound during their time behind the desk but only allowed it to reach full fruition on the fantastic *Intoxicated Demons* EP. In an era when hip-hop design started shedding its myopic fixation on bad gold chains and bad haircuts the sleeve to *Intoxicated Demons* was key, hijacking Hank Mobley's original Blue Note cover art to knowing effect. The music within simply tore your head off, perhaps the most inventive use of obscure loops and samples and filthy rugged beats this side of Premo and Pete Rock.

Beatnuts always framed their rhymes with incredibly complex yet utterly immediate music. Together these elements made for warped, wonderful, lurid, lucid music. Home, you felt, is what they drew from the most, Corona, its streets – the Beatnuts were unique at the time for the notion of sampling themselves and their kids and their neighbourhood rather than stealing dialogue and sounds purely from obvious old funk records and movies. It gives *Intoxicated Demons* and all their production work a clammy realness that rubs against the alien strangeness of some of their sources in wondrous juxtaposition. Oft forgot when people think about the East Coast. Never forget 'em.

Column 15

68 91 **Ch** Cypress Hill		
69 94 **Di** D.I.T.C.	**74 93** **Wu** Wu-Tang Clan	**79 94** **O** Outkast
70 93 **Ak** Alkaholiks	**75 95** **Ra** Raekwon	**80 97** **Lj** Lil Jon
71 92 **R** Redman	**76 95** **Gz** GZA	**81 95** **Mp** Master P
72 92 **St** Steve Rifkind	**77 96** **Rl** Real Live	**82 94** **Ds** DJ Screw
73 93 **B** Beatnuts	**78 93** **Rz** RZA	**83 97** **Jd** J Dilla

WU-TANG CLAN

Still the sound of an alien invasion. Hip hop is joined up, but sometimes takes the ground from under you. Such was your feeling when 'Protect Ya Neck' and then *Enter The Wu-Tang* crashed into your life in late 1992 and early 1993. Who the hell? What the fuck? What weird corner of the universe did these psychos call home?

Home was Staten Island, the most neglected of the five boros, an isolation that had clearly enforced a tangential development at exponential speed with the Wu. Nothing sounded like them: these were rhymes unlike anyone else's, a dizzying dazzling run of metaphor, allusion, stream-of-consciousness visionary poetics and sudden brute real talk. Once you'd heard them you craved more.

The Wu pulled nothing short of a coup on hip hop. Stylistically, it was the most complete concept since Public Enemy – a union of look, language and intent fused in ancient martial arts ideas (discipline, brotherhood, technique) and put in the Shaolin Staten present. The Clan appeared as faceless assassins on the sleeve, and that perfect sublime logo soon was everywhere and became imprinted in your mind forever.

Wu-Tang were a collective of nine MCs who accepted a deal with BMG only on the implicit understanding that each would be able to work as solo artists. Together they made *Enter The Wu-Tang* with main-ideas man and producer RZA. Music so bizarre it frequently failed to resemble music. Deeply atmospheric, slathered with kung-fu sound FX and dialogue culled from Run Run Shaw grindhouse movies, rugged primitivist funk and ghostly distorted samples, eerie loops and nightmarish echo-plexed dub gave their music a dread ambience. Perhaps the strangest hip-hop music to ever gain mainstream acceptance, it was a signpost to a future of infinite possibility. The follow up LP, *Wu-Tang Forever*, was lambasted as a sprawling mess. It is, but it's also the greatest nineties hip-hop LP of all and Wu-Tang Clan were the second greatest rap group ever after Public Enemy.

RAEKWON

By 1995, the Wu were in demand worldwide, Method Man and Ol' Dirty Bastard had even taken the pop-dollar and cameo'd on tracks by Mary J. Blige and Mariah Carey. Both had also released incredible albums in their own right, Method's *Tical* and ODB's *Return To The 36 Chambers*. Just when you feared the Wu might be in danger of diluting their special hold on you, out came the greatest solo LP any of them gave us, Raekwon's *Only Built 4 Cuban Linx...* Recasting the Clan as an assortment of coked-out Goodfellas (Meth became Johnny Blaze, Ghostface became Tony Starks, RZA was Bobby Steele, Master Killa was Noodles and even Nas got a cameo as Nas Escobar) and introducing the incredible new members of the Wu-Tang family (Sunz of Man and Cappadonna), it was an immense record most of us haven't yet managed to fully grasp. Segued together with an impenetrable flow of John Woo samples and turbid streams of street dialogue, the whole album recreated the urban heat and cruel waste it so perfectly described lyrically. There are moments here when you're left frozen and stranded wondering what the hell is going on. There is the insane acid rock and diseased psychedelia of 'Glaciers of Ice' and 'Verbal Intercourse', with its immaculate rhyming, impossible richness of imagery and density of content. *Cuban Linx* was something you couldn't leave alone, couldn't stop exploring, something that still confers a pall of inferiority on much of the rest of rap every time you hear it. As a seamless continuum of beat and rhyme, it was the Clan's most flawless production yet. As one gigantic challenge to the rap world (and indeed, the entire pop universe) it still remains unanswered.

GZA

The Wu member with the longest prior experience in hip hop (signed and had an album out before even joining the crew) curiously released probably the weirdest most whacked-out solo project of all the Clan. On *Liquid Swords*, released in late 1995, RZA's psychedelic reach was given full scope, ran wild on wide-open spaces in possibly his most eclectic and eye-popping production yet. Once again, as *Cuban Linx* had, GZA recast the Clan (U God became Lucky Hands, Inspectah Deck became Roily Fingers) and introduced phenomenal new talents from the Wu stable (Life, Dreddy Kruger and the scarifyingly good Killah Priest).

Liquid Swords immediately established itself as the most accessibly funky Wu album. GZA pulls some astonishing vocal tricks, and the threaded motif of dialogue from the infamous samurai Lone Wolf movies is a linking idea of sheer genius, much as John Woo's *The Killer* held *Cuban Linx* together so well.

What was so amazing and so encouraging about the solo LPs was the unity and individuality they balanced so well, the feeling that there was so much more of this stuff to come. You couldn't simply find a space for Wu-Tang in your schedule, make a lifestyle choice, file them away in a corner of your world. They were too total, their demands on you too huge to negotiate without obsession. They seeped into your body, affected your mind, burrowed into your soul, and coloured your whole experience. Only hip hop can do this. Only Wu can do hip hop like this.

77 96
RI
Real Live

REAL LIVE

As soon as the Wu broke out of their Staten Island stronghold they started guesting on other crews' records, particularly artists that had influenced them and whom they respected. Mobb Deep, Redman, AZ, Busta Rhymes, Kool G Rap and others were all blessed by Wu cameos but perhaps the finest affiliates were Real Live, a duo from New York. Their producer, K-Def, had learned his chops from Marley Marl while working on the Lords of the Underground's classic *Here Come The Lords* LP. *Real Live: The Turnaround* featured guest-spots from

Cappadonna and Ghostface Killah from the Wu-Tang Clan, and is a shamefully unknown highpoint of New York Golden-Age hip hop.

Like the Wu-Tang Clan, Real Live told crime stories, and suffused their tales with a cinematic eye for drama and staging. This was hip-hop noir par excellence, peopled with figures as doomed as a James Ellroy hero. K-Def arranged the album with an almost symphonic breadth of tone and colour. You can feel the steam seeping from the streets, the smog between the beats, the rain and the neon and the bloodstains and the cocaine.

NYC hip hop was reaching a peak it would never attain again, a dead end albeit a wonderful one, a dead end that also threw up masterpieces like Blahzay Blahzay's *Blah Blah Blah*, Company Flow's *Funcrusher Plus* and Organized Konfusion's *Stress: The Extinction Agenda*. This was an unrepeatable zenith for hip hop but, by 1998, tired of the coasts, rap wanted to take a cross-country tour. It pointed its nose away from old New York and headed down south.

RZA

78	93
Rz	
RZA	

Like all shifts in hip hop, the sound RZA created was beyond fusing familiar sounds to create a new whole. RZA brought completely new sounds to the mixing desk, and then mashed them together in an order, shape and mood you couldn't reproduce with an infinite number of monkeys, unlimited turntables and an eternity to play with. From the brutal murk of 'Bring Da Ruckus', the smoky funk of 'Shame On A Nigga', through the lush insanity of 'Clan In Da Front', 'C.R.E.A.M.' and 'Tearz', to the staggering distorto-groove of '7th Chamber', *Enter the Wu-Tang* shocked hip hop back to life. It changed the lexicon of word and sound that the form could investigate, and crucially, was the first LP in too long that you learned by heart, that you let infect your everyday walk and talk.

RZA hated samples. He'd use one note and change it into noise, put those noises together over heavy drums to a formula only he and the rest of the Wu understood. He didn't want to show his face, just infect people with pure sound they could put their own pictures to. The first of the Wu to exercise their contractual freedom, he broke out in 1994 to create the Gravediggaz masterpiece *Niggamortis*, an unrepeatable classic that both invented and immolated an entirely new genre, horror-core. On all of the early Wu-related releases you can hear RZA absolutely bucking the old populism/innovation dichotomies, creating intensely avant-garde music that just happened to be the biggest sound in rap. It was RZA's production and vision that gave the Wu a power and potential unheard of in rap history, reaching for this writer a zenith on the epic, deranging *Wu-Tang Forever*.

Diaspora

Up until now in this book, hip hop has been at some remove from the mainstream, always in danger of being co-opted by pop or other genres. It is the alternative music most prone to pillage.

But by the late nineties hip hop is generating such massive revenues, is embedded so deep in the mainstream culture of the US that it flips its role entirely. From here on in, hip hop willingly pimps itself to pop, and it performs the same vampiric moves on underground culture as the mainstream culture had once enacted on hip hop itself. This is also accompanied by hip hop extending its reach and range beyond its East Coast and West Coast archetypes and investigating local, regional scenes, then co-opting and feeding that local 'heat' back into mainstream hip hop. Bounce music is a great example of this.

'Bounce' was a type of New Orleans club dance music popular among Nola's large LGBT and drag communities. It was heavy on slogans and back and forth Mardi-Gras-style chanting and up-tempo beats. As a spin on hip hop it most closely resembled Old-School hip hop. Lyrics were here only used to keep rumps shaking, the music was usually of brute effective simplicity, frequently based on one of two beats, the 'Brown Beat' from Derek B's bounce-staple 'Rock The Beat' and the 'Triggerman' beat, rather incongruously pulled from Old-School Queens duo the Showboys's 1986 track 'Drag Rap'. Local New Orleans DJs like DJ Jubilee brought the form out on sporadic 12 inches but it was really just a live music form, with its own dance-moves like twerkin' and p-popping, its own clubs and a determinedly New Orleans club fan base.

When the superb Juvenile brought it to mainstream attention via tracks like 'Back That Azz Up' the split between the roots of Bounce and the way that hip hop co-opted it meant that the scene in Nola hardened into Sissy Bounce, determinedly gay and proud and unpalatable to the overwhelmingly homophobic nature of so much hip hop.

Swiftly the Southern explosion in hip hop ran through the same cycle hip hop had already gone through on the coasts. Witness the change in Southern rap music upon the dawn of 'trap music'. A nebulous concept to grasp but 'Southern ambient' comes closest, I feel. Made with a tiny complement of instruments (mainly 808 and Pro Tools) and a tiny set of effects (synthetic string/brass stabs) and featuring a tiny cast of characters (thugs, criminals, hoodlums, bitches), Trap emerges as a kind of new essentially limited fable of the South. Lyrics were entirely preoccupied with backyard criminality and the day-to-day flexings and retreats of the ego demanded by that criminal life. A polyglot sound that grows out of Lil Jon's 'crunk'-style, but that mixed that music's up-tempo party-orientated nature with the sound of slo-mo Houston-style screwed-beats and ended up being the go-to sound of choice for mainstream artists seeking a bit of reflected street-heat.

Partly Trap's built-in capacity for decadence and diffusion, the way its sonic limitations and lyrical myopia can be simulated and conjured with such minimum effort by other genres and artists, set the seal on its own demise and theft but the speed of Trap's re-appropriation and dilution has been dizzying, everyone from Beyoncé to Lady Gaga trying it out. Trap is the moment where the Southern rap explosion of the noughties finds itself washed up on its own bleak shore, gasping for air. I suspect we'll be watching its gills twitch to an asphyxiated halt for some time yet. Crucially, the migration and spread of rap serves to make local scenes hotbeds of an ever-rotating cast of new names. Steadily, calmly floating above this turbid underground, New York and Hollywood re-emerge as the real power bases of rap royalty, Jay, Dre and Eminem becoming wealthy in ways previously undreamed of in hip hop. The traditional superstructure of hip hop, initially threatened by the diaspora, hardens and ossifies. The South, eventually, did not rise again.

Column 16

74 93 **Wu** Wu-Tang Clan	79 94 **O** Outkast	84 96 **Jz** Jay-Z
75 95 **Ra** Raekwon	80 97 **Lj** Lil Jon	85 99 **Em** Eminem
76 95 **Gz** GZA	81 95 **Mp** Master P	86 97 **Me** Missy Elliott
77 96 **Rl** Real Live	82 94 **Ds** DJ Screw	87 95 **Ro** Roots
78 93 **Rz** RZA	83 97 **Jd** J Dilla	88 95 **N** Neptunes
		89 97 **T** Timbaland

OUTKAST

79		94
	O	
	Outkast	

By the late nineties, hip hop could no longer be seen as a music confined to LA and NYC, it was a music that was popping off across the world. Previously neglected regional scenes started getting worldwide attention with a proliferation of unique local styles exploding out of the industrial heartland and the Bible Belt South of the US, massively expanding what hip hop could sound like and what it could mean. Perhaps the first non-coastal major city to impact on hip hop in a big way in this period was Atlanta, where LaFace records, started out in the city by legendary New Jack Swing producers L.A. Reid and Babyface Edmonds, expanded their R'n'B roster, which had already scored major hits by Toni Braxton and TLC to include some of the unique nascent hip-hop talent on the Atlanta scene.

LaFace's most inventive act, Outkast, made music unlike anything else going on in rap at the time. They were influenced by Miami bass, LA G-funk, heavily reliant on the 808, and touched with all kinds of sweet Southern soul textures and harmonies. Organized Noise are the emblematic production crew of Atlanta's hip-hop explosion, Goodie Mob's 'Soul Food' their definitive production, but it's Outkast who took the template the furthest to create perhaps the most stunning body of work in modern rap. Their high-point, the utterly spellbinding *Speakerboxxx/The Love Below* released in 2003, remains hip hop's biggest selling album ever, thanks to 'Hey Ya!' being a smash but also thanks to the duo's incredible schizophrenic talents in production and lyricism. Atlanta would stay at the heart of hip hop's regional explosion thanks to the energy, charm and plain populist freakiness of its later sons, T.I. Lil Jon and his crunk disciples and Ludacris's Disturbing tha Peace crew. Whether that energy translated into much salvageable good music is a question we'll be repeatedly confronted with over the course of the ensuing elements. But as defined by Outkast, 'Southern rap' created some of the new millennium's most innovative and remarkable music. Long may they wander through their own wonder.

LIL JON

In 1995, Outkast and Goodie Mob were famously booed at the *Source* magazine awards show, condescendingly looked at as hicks by the New York crowd. Outkast picked up the Best New Group award. Their debut LP *Southernplayalisticadillacmusik* had gone platinum in a year. Outkast and their generation of Southern rappers explored Southern identity through the cadence of their words and the sound of their music. 'Dirty South' hip hop, as it started to be called, was accessible but also innovative and explored the more troubling side of the South's racial politics.

The wave of crunk rap that followed was pioneered by Lil Jon and Three 6 Mafia and was more focused on making Southern identity an all-inclusive identity, linked more to a lucratively general aspirational set of commodities and behaviours: partying, bling, weed, booze, bitches.

Crunk music, an 808-heavy mix of Old-School Miami bass, Baltimore and Memphis club music, was the tool, the buzzword that Lil Jon and others used to enact this takeover but really the key is the slipperiness of the 'crunk' term. It rapidly lost any etymological surety and wound up being applied as a signifier of a new, deliberately inarticulate hedonism in black hip-hop culture, more akin to the techno and house scenes than anything that had previously occurred in rap (crunk artists didn't really rap, they shouted). By 2002, nearly two-thirds of the rap charts were made up of Southern artists, unthinkable a decade earlier when Outkast were getting booed off the *Source* stage. By the time Outkast won Grammys in 2004, the Dirty South had become a marketing ploy, a culture industry that had in effect Southernised American hip hop. Mainly to hip hop's lasting damage.

MASTER P

81   95
Mp
Master P

The Big Easy's long exclusion and isolation from hip hop looks more and more strange and unfathomable the longer you look at it, but until Mystikal signed for Jive in 1995, it's tricky to think of any New Orleans artists who'd broken for the coasts and made it. This was partly down to sheer geographical distance, but you also sense that, culturally, New Orleans is a city that likes keeping itself to itself, unwilling to compromise itself artistically or let any out-of-town operators steal its unique style. Two labels changed the story in the mid-nineties: No Limit Records and Cash Money.

In 1995, Master P brought his No Limit label from California back to his hometown New Orleans. He inked a distribution deal with Priority and boosted the profile of No Limit Records by picking up Snoop Dogg after he'd acrimoniously left Death Row. Pretty soon everything they brought out was a hit. No Limit's recipe for success was to provide a glut of very similar music based on New Orleans bounce music. The albums were indistinguishable musically and visually thanks to their Pen and Pixel sleeves (the Houston design company who created the look of Dirty South hip hop with their sleeves for No Limit). Hip hop was recast back to being purely party music, low on lyrical content, high on energy. Albums were crazy-long, cheaply packaged, packed with cameos from No Limit's growing roster. No Limit was the Dirty South label par excellence.

The Williams brothers' Cash Money label repeated the No Limit template with even greater success, thanks to the fact they actually had some great talent like Juvenile, and had a more discerning sense of artists relations, signing Nicki Minaj, Drake and Lil Wayne and diversifying into the successful Young Money imprint. Through Cash Money and No Limit Records, New Orleans didn't just put itself on the hip-hop map, it became a model of how to generate big cash from minimum investment.

82		94
	Ds	
	DJ Screw	

DJ SCREW

Substances have always had an effect on hip hop, whether it's the ever-present weed that accompanies its production or the business executives' favourite, cocaine. In the late nineties and early noughties, hip hop opened itself up to substances it hadn't hit so hard before, including ecstasy and home-brewed prescription-based concoctions. These new drugs changed and refracted the hip-hop sound. Before the nineties, most Southern hip hop was fast. Houston's DJ Screw bucked that trend with his 'Chopped and Screwed' remix style, slowing beats down to a somnambulist 60bpm, tweaking the pitch down until it resembled a slow-motion stroll through jelly, perfect for jeeps, perfect for allowing rappers to make their rapping more conversational, more story-based, more suitable for the burning hot Texas sun. It suited Houston's favourite new drug, Purple Drank, which was a concoction of sweets, fizzy pop and codeine-heavy cough-syrup. It left users initially euphoric then steadily drowsy and fuzzy. Purple Drank circumvented Texas's tough drug laws but it was highly addictive and indirectly led to the death of DJ Screw himself.

DJ Screw's sound percolated through to everyone in the Southern hip-hop explosion and can still be heard on innumerable mix-tapes and albums today. Remember kids, winners don't do drugs.

83		97
	Jd	
	J Dilla	

J DILLA

And yet, and yet, and yet, you'd be deranged to think hip hop's move from the coasts inland was all in the direction of hip hop becoming, once again, purely party music. Detroit's J Dilla had something to bring to hip hop that no one else could quite match, a production that was equal parts street-tough and magically imaginative, a glorious agglomeration of what had passed before him and a pathway out of all that lineage to an entirely new garden of delights. As synthetic and plastic as Flash and Mantronik, as densely layered and entangling as the Bomb Squad and Marley Marl, as freaky and fucked up as Beatnuts and K-Def, but always sharpened with his own eye and hands and lysergic vision. Inevitably, after people heard his debut production, Slum Village's first album *Fantastic Voyage*, J Dilla was instantly in demand across rap and pop for people wanting to tap into that album's stealthy mix of ear-popping and smooth sounds. In the epic discography he notched up in his too-short life, I'd go for two albums in particular: *Champion Sound*, the album he created with Madlib in 2003, and *Donuts*, the instrumental beats-album that emerged just three days before his premature death in 2006.

The assumption among many that J Dilla is merely a hero for the indie-rap fans isn't just damaging to his legacy, it overlooks how connected most hip hoppers are with J Dilla, just how well known this supposedly 'experimental' music is among hip hop's fans in the clubs and on the street. For the longest time you'd hear J Dilla beats out of passing windows. Dilla's lo-fi open-minded production methods, his speed of work (which led to an enormous backlog of unreleased tracks brought out posthumously) and his colossal impatience with the lumbering slowness of traditional industry structures made him an evergreen inspiration for everyone bringing out innovative hip-hop music unconcerned with mainstream success. If you want to hear where his music has ended up, check out releases on labels like Brick, Mello Music Group, Fat Beats, Britain's YNR and Big Dada records. They are all labels that, on the quiet, are intent on hip hop remaining a progressive and inventive music.

Column 17

		90 **04** **Kw** Kanye West

79 **94** **O** Outkast	**84** **96** **Jz** Jay-Z	**91** **07** **Nm** Nicki Minaj
80 **97** **Lj** Lil Jon	**85** **99** **Em** Eminem	**92** **10** **Kl** Kendrick Lamar
81 **95** **Mp** Master P	**86** **97** **Me** Missy Elliott	**93** **08** **Of** Odd Future
82 **94** **Ds** DJ Screw	**87** **95** **Ro** Roots	**94** **11** **Ck** Chief Keef
83 **97** **Jd** J Dilla	**88** **95** **N** Neptunes	
	89 **97** **T** Timbaland	

JAY-Z

Everything about Jay-Z in 2015 is meant to dazzle and render you dumb with the inarguable figures. As a commercial fact he can obliterate all sense when talking of his musical worth. The Roc-A-Fella dynasty is testament to his untrammelled hunger to be the biggest rap star on the planet. He's become his own marketing tool, spawning a clothing line, liquor brands, sports bars, beauty products, footwear shops, Hollywood films and, every now and then, music. *Reasonable Doubt* from 1996 remains his greatest moment but since that debut he's stayed at the top with suburbanite MTV viewers, inner-city hip-hop fans, and the critics. He's sharp and bellicose enough to squash doubters, see out rivals, rarely breaking a sweat. He sailed through hip hop's interminable beef-years despite ruckuses with Nas and Mobb Deep, and ensured that when he needed to behave himself to keep out of jail he did. At all times, like Russell Simmons, he's been looking round the corner, doing whatever it takes to stay ahead of the curve. Unlike Russell Simmons you do get the feeling with Jay-Z that for all his other roles as CEO and entrepreneur and brand-manager and consultant, hip-hop and rapping are what he enjoys most, what he would like to focus on most. But how do you become an artist again when you've spent so long ensuring you're a brand? Eventually he's going to have to start bringing music out again that doesn't just reference the older work that made him famous. Or perhaps he'll just sit on his half-a-billion dollars, and leave the younger talent to take his place. As he himself said, 'Would you rather be underpaid or overrated?'

EMINEM

The hip-hop Elvis, with all the contradictions and problems that entails. Without a doubt, Eminem is one of the most overrated rappers this side of Tupac in hip hop's tableaux of official superstars. A Dre protégé, Marshall

Mathers from Missouri spent his childhood shuttled between St Joseph, his hometown, and Detroit. By 14 he was performing raps, building his rep doing battle-rhymes in clubs. Family deaths and births kept putting hiatuses in Em's career and the bitterness he'd feel about his family could be expressed through his Slim Shady alter-ego. After getting a silver medal in 1997's LA Rap Olympics MC Battle, a tape found its way to Interscope CEO Jimmy Iovine and Dre.

There's no denying that the early singles were kind of thrilling, as novelties, like Bubba Sparxxx or Ludacris. Midwestern hooliganism of the first order. Pretty soon, though, hip-hop fans stopped listening and Eminem's fan base became composed of an entirely different kind of music fan, overwhelmingly suburban and the kind of middle-class audience that can turn a brilliant battle-rapper (which Em undeniably is) into an economic juggernaut. Stretched over yawning albums his short sharp talent wilts fast. He's here in this book, like Jay-Z, less for his music than for the hegemonising effect he's had on the culture. Labels look for the next Mathers or the next Carter, and ignore every other possibility.

MISSY ELLIOTT

In total contrast to everyone above her in this column, Missy is the late nineties, early noughties star whom I think is the most criminally underrated. A brilliant rapper, arranger and producer in her own right, it was her hook up with Virginia's R'n'B production genius Timbaland that led to one of the strongest runs of singles and albums in late nineties rap, from *Supa Dupa Fly* through to the mind-blowing *Miss E... So Addictive* and *Under Construction*, and I'd say she created the greatest body of work in post Golden-Age hip hop next to Outkast. On tracks like 'Slide', 'Ain't That Funny', 'Gossip Folks' and 'Work It' she and Timbaland created a unique high-point in the post SP-1200 sounds of rap. Murderously addictive, sonically gorgeous, irresistibly physical, deeply cerebral, these are records that, along with Aaliyah's Timba-productions, still sound like the future. She did all this without compromise, using unforgettable videos to play with her image in delightful subversion of traditional rap female stereotypes. Always able to expand her music in whatever direction her imagination saw fit, her relative disappearance into production was a great loss, although gratifyingly the female presence in rap music has been growing ever since. If hip hop is going to change, way more women have to get involved on the creative side. If it doesn't happen I give the music 10 years before it's dead.

ROOTS

87   95
Ro
Roots

If you'd only known about the Roots from their initial press you might have avoided them without knowing that they use live instruments absolutely not for reasons of muso credibility. In 1987, when rapper Black Thought and drummer ?uestlove became friends at the Philadelphia High School for Performing Arts, the duo had no money for the DJ essentials of turntables, mics, mixers and vinyl. So they recreated hip-hop tracks with ?uestlove's drum kit backing Black Thought's rhymes. Playing around school and the sidewalk and talent shows they started to earn money and hooked up with bassist Hub and rapper Malik B. Their debut LP for MCA *Do You Want More?!!!??!* forsook usual hip-hop protocol and was produced without any samples or pre-recorded material. Sharpening their blazing live show on the Lollapalooza rock/rap package festival circuit, the Roots hired Rahzel (a beat-boxer who'd worked with Flash and Cool J) and Scott Storch to beef up their sound and *Illadelph Halflife*, released in 1996, became a real leap-off point, a startlingly honest look at keeping a band together through industry ignorance and touring madness, shot through with music that sampled their live performances but was as spectral and suggestive as Outkast. By the time of *Things Fall Apart* in 1999, they'd located a bold, new space in hip hop. Abstract, part studio-spun, part live-heat, the Roots always dealt in a more ambiguous, politicised engagement with the problems in the age. They remain a downer-ed yet uplifting, fearsomely intelligent yet forlorn inspiration for anyone daring to think hip hop can still be art.

NEPTUNES AND TIMBALAND

The Neptunes and Timbaland were producers who came from Virginia Beach, were sired by Teddy Riley (who happened to set up a recording studio right next to the boys' school) and who changed the sound of late nineties rap music. These were producers keen to bring hip hop's reliance on seventies funk on a few years, and started tapping the oddity of Prince, the harshness of New Jack Swing, and the explosion in regional dance scenes for a new way for hip hop to sound. Though different in style one thing united them in their productions – a sense of wobbliness, introduced not just through their unique choice of samples (often from Middle Eastern or Bollywood recordings which gave both Timba and Neptunes productions a sense of exotica and non-adhesion to normal four-bar pop) but through their beats. In a normal hip-hop production the beat is steady, slower than the rap that would go on top of it – the music couches the words. In a Neptunes or Timba production the opposite occurs – the music punctures the words, the beat is as busy and syncopated as the voice. The seemingly effortless, identikit nature of Neptunes and Timbaland productions became the go-to sound for a wealth of rappers seeking to push their careers in new directions in the late nineties. You went to Timbaland for a surefire hit, the Neptunes for an image change. As perfected on Clipse's *Grindin'*, Missy's *Under Construction* and N.E.R.D.'s *In Search Of*, these Virginia Beach productions were state-of-the-art. Only Pharrell has survived with any visibility. Like most hip-hop stars of the modern age, he remains busy making plain the fact he never needs to work again.

Column 18

	90 04 **Kw** Kanye West
84 96 **Jz** Jay-Z	91 07 **Nm** Nicki Minaj
85 99 **Em** Eminem	92 10 **Kl** Kendrick Lamar
86 97 **Me** Missy Elliott	93 08 **Of** Odd Future
87 95 **Ro** Roots	94 11 **Ck** Chief Keef
88 95 **N** Neptunes	
89 97 **T** Timbaland	

KANYE WEST

90 04
Kw
Kanye West

The most common question asked when rap fans gather now is 'Is hip hop dead?' Dumb question. In a strict sense, of course it is. Despite revivalists, retronauts and the fetishisation of old artefacts and practice by ageing hip-hop fans, kids aren't b-boying, graffing, turntablising like they used to. Elements of the original culture are falling into dilapidation. Rap music, initially just one of the four pillars, has become equated with hip hop for most people, especially the kids vital in keeping any culture alive. Rap music is healthier than ever in terms of participation, in terms of its pull on kids worldwide as an expressive way out of the lives they have, a promise that they can use the lives they have to get themselves a different life.

Kanye is not just the biggest name in this millennium's rap music but also the most entertaining, the most controversial, the most vexing, and the artist who still makes that transformative power of rap most apparent. West's arrogance is legendary. His seemingly unerring belief in his own immortal greatness is immune to critique or outright calumny. But what can't be denied him is that he's made some of the most compelling contributions to hip-hop culture ever since that culture got blasted apart, spread thin and returned to being a mere technique and detail of pop. Spotted by Jay-Z, hired by Roc-A-Fella, initially dissuaded from rapping, it would've been easy for West to settle into a career and dotage of pure production but the man has something to say. Like any middle-class person into hip-hop, to a certain extent, he has to invent his hurdles, set up barriers so he can bust them down. But he's gone above and beyond simply creating himself a career. In his albums, he's telling an utterly engrossing story of how we confront sexuality and race in the Internet age; musically he seems utterly unconcerned with shoring up the past, paying dues or being correct. What's thrilling about West's music, particularly on his two true masterpieces

808s & Heartbreak and *Yeezus*, is that he's firmly focused on carving out a future for hip hop, a future that if anything harks back most to those open-ended early years when rap was both an uptown funk and a downtown art, close to the avant-garde. He has some astonishing rhymes, real rude-boy genius. Thrillingly he wants to make hip hop both utterly experimental but also stadium-sized, the soundtrack of modernity, central to the understanding of *now*. We shouldn't let the day-to-day nuttiness of the 'figure' blind us to just what a staggering thing *Yeezus* is. Jam 'Black Skinhead' on loud and hear hip hop burn itself a new future.

NICKI MINAJ

91   07

Nm

Nicki Minaj

Because of the Internet, the way that rap is created and put out has never been more globally democratised. The way the entertainment industries drains the life out of that dizzyingly vast rap culture has never been more ruthless, lucrative or restrictive to the unmediated free street-level innovations that still make it the greatest music on earth. Minaj is here, like Eminem, not because of the quality of her work but because she's so emblematic of the process of commodification and dilution that passes for a hip-hop career now. Like Drake, Curren$y and J. Cole in the latter noughties, Minaj brought out a series of fantastic mix-tapes that heralded to hipped cognoscenti a great new talent. We all went and downloaded them from Datpiff for free and marvelled at the ease and venom with which she flowed, the thoughtfulness, the music's subtle unsubtlety, the lyrical transgression. Then, fatally, she got signed to a record label. Almost immediately, just as occurred with Drake and Curren$y and J. Cole, a strange timidity started creeping into her music. You'd think that signing to a major might sharpen your music up. The reverse occurs for nearly all artists making that step up from Internet notoriety to mainstream distribution. They must aim for mass appeal. They must have popular and famous guests. So every album must contain far too many cameos, far too many producers. That sense of rolling with collaborators and a whole crew of like-minds actually ends up obscuring the persona who should be at the heart of it, hiding the fact they have nothing to say. Minaj's saving grace is her humour – too often in mainstream modern rap, 'fun' is not allowed, humour has been eliminated, a self-pitying seriousness is the default setting. Still, Minaj hasn't made an interesting record since she stopped making mix-tapes. Nor has Curren$y, Drake or J. Cole. That's the choice on offer these days for young artists: make art and stay poor; make dross and get rich. The industry's done playing Mr Nice Guy. It's now proud to be a rapaciously ravenous charnel-house of aspiration. We're still, slowly, agonisingly, losing a generation down its monstrous craw. The sooner this superstructure gets destroyed, the sooner rap music can start playing in its ruins.

KENDRICK LAMAR

Kids still want to call what they do 'rap music'. Why is that? Because they know that by moving on and making the old sound ever-older they are participating in a culture called rap, a culture that gives them a response to their realities with more freedom, more fury, more possibilities than any other art form. The Ferguson riots and the rash of highly public police brutality cases in the middle of America's twenty-fourth decade posed questions to black America, and Kendrick Lamar's *To Pimp A Butterfly* was rap's most cogent, dazzling response. It could be seen as a moment where radical politics and radical music returned to rap and R'n'B precisely at the time it was most needed. A breath-taking appraisal of the broken promises and bloody pathways in and out of America's heartland malaise, *To Pimp A Butterfly* was seen by many as an act of recovery, a bringing back to rap of its social conscience. That's emphatically not the way it sounds though. It's a far more futurist album than it is a look back. If it does tip the wink to any antecedents it's definitely the Afro-futurist likes of Sun Ra and P-funk rather than anything purely related to rap music, as well as a sweet soulful Curtis Mayfield/Gil Scott-Heron sense of love as political act. If Public Enemy's Chuck D once nailed rap music's role as 'CNN for black people' then Lamar is making the most useful rap music of his generation, improvisatory, intelligent, incisive, inspirational. It's as laceratingly self-critical and questioning of Lamar himself as it is lethally dangerous to precisely the racial and class divides that form the bedrock for rap's current pimping out. Anyone saying rap is dead should hear it. In Lamar and West, it's clearly in rude health.

ODD FUTURE

93   **08**

Of

Odd Future

No matter how justified complainants are about what's 'gone wrong' with rap, they're almost all invariably old, slightly out of touch and harking for a passed irretrievable age, a dead giveaway of their own conservatism and superannuation. Hip hop may be dead, rap music *cannot be stopped*. There will always be at least a dozen reasons a week to keep listening.

In the Internet age, hiding yourself, only revealing shards and fragments over time to build a sense of intrigue is nigh on impossible. When someone, or something, manages this it's a rare delight indeed and it's something that LA hip-hop collective Odd Future Wolf Gang Kill Them All (or OFWGKTA) perfected. A loose-limbed collective of kids, skaters, artists, filmmakers, MCs and beat-makers, what was most startling about them wasn't that they were seasoned veterans playing a wise-assed game in reinvention, or pop intellectuals putting together a hip collage. OFWGKTA were genuinely kids – not Disney kids or showbiz kids or even kids with a dream, but kids with nightmares. A 10-strong Crenshaw-born crew of readers, ranters and rapscallions they defied categorisation, created their own new blueprints every time they dropped, and though they seemed almost designed to tick boxes for critics, they hoodwinked and out-thought those critics every step of the way. Music that makes you feel old, music where you have to stop talking and listen, and read, and watch, and wake up to *their* Cooper-black-fonted world.

Crucially beyond their musical and visual genius, OFWGKTA, in their inclusiveness, contained a blueprint that might still just be rap's way into a new future. When affiliate Frank Ocean came out of the closet it was a pivotal moment in rap history, lifting the lid on a welter of queer-rap that had been neglected. It suggested that, for hip hop to move on, it would have to join the modern world in rejecting, or at least questioning, the misogyny, homophobia and macho masculinity that had been its world up until then. Like Lamar, Odd Future's work knew how tied in patriarchy and racism were and questioned that relationship, questioned rap's quiescence in that enduring history of oppression. As long as rap remains a music where crews like Odd Future and Death Grips can find expression, it will remain, just as it's always been, the most infinitely suggestive music on the planet: outsider music, rebel music, for the forgotten.

CHIEF KEEF

Drill is a defiantly gothic take on Trap, blotting out the sunshine, replacing it with darker menacing skies, a more intense claustrophobia thanks to its roots in Chicago (or 'Chir-aq' as Drill god Chief Keef would have it), and an even more pervasive feel of violence. Hyper-aggressive lyrics and martial gunfire-strafed beats reflect the dizzying murder statistics and the ever-present threat of police-sanctioned homicide that characterises the modern American black urban space. The voices of Drill are detached, nonchalant, nihilistic, numbed in direct contradiction to Chicago's more elderly history of conscious rap. Where the first wave of gangsta-rap contained at least a thread of social justice, animated by the LA riots, Drill rap resists nothing, celebrates crime, dehumanises victims as if they were so much *Grand Theft Auto* detail. For a tight scene what's most apparent is the total lack of community spirit; rivals are to be shamed, not pitied, past bonds of togetherness forgotten and mocked and deserted just as the kids who make and listen to Drill have been deserted and forgotten. Rap music, at the point of hip-hop culture's death, is still stepping in and proving to again be music for the isolated, estranged. It is music for outsiders, music that shocks the elite, music that doesn't have to enable a sense of belonging but that can render an individual's isolation. Far more interestingly that the 'cloud-rap' phenomenon of recent East Coast rap, Drill's Midwestern morbidity and menace is the most compelling playing out of rap's retreat inward from the coasts. Whether it can keep itself hid is rap's next battleground.

Select discography

Pre-Hip Hop Gil Scott-Heron *Small Talk At 125th & Lenox, Pieces Of A Man*

Iceberg Slim *Reflections*

James Brown *Say It Loud I'm Black And I'm Proud, Ain't It Funky, Hot Pants, There It Is, The Payback, Hell*

Last Poets *The Last Poets, This Is Madness*

Lightning Rod *Hustlers Convention*

Parliament/Funkadelic *Cosmic Slop, Up For The Down Stroke, Mothership Connection, Motor Booty Affair, Tales Of Kidd Funkadelic, The Clones Of Dr Funkenstein, Funktelechy Vs The Placebo Syndrome*

Richard Pryor *That Nigger's Crazy, Bicentennial Nigger*

Sly and the Family Stone *Stand!, There's A Riot Goin' On, Fresh*

Watts Prophets *Rappin' Black In A White World, Black Voices, On The Streets in Watts*

Old School Afrika Bambaataa 'Zulu Nation Throwdown', 'Jazzy Sensation', 'Planet Rock', 'Looking For The Perfect Beat'

Cold Crush Brothers *All The Way Live In '82*

Grandmaster Flash & Melle Mel 'White Lines'

Grand Wizard Theodore & the Fantastic Five 'Can I Get A Soul Clap'

Grandmaster Flash & the Furious Five 'Superappin', *The Message*

Kurtis Blow *Kurtis Blow*

Treacherous Three 'The New Rap Language', 'The Body Rock', 'At The Party'

Various Artists *The Sugar Hill Story – Old School Rap To The Beat Y'all*

Various Artists *Live Convention '82*

Various Artists *Wild Style*

Various Artists *The Great Rap Hits*

Various Artists *The Third Unheard*
Various Artists: *Big Apple Rappin': The Early Days Of Hip-Hop Culture In New York City 1979–1982*

New School

Beastie Boys *Licensed To Ill, Paul's Boutique, Check Your Head*
Big Daddy Kane *Long Live The Kane, It's A Big Daddy Thing*
Biz Markie *Goin' Off*
Boogie Down Productions *Criminal Minded, By All Means Necessary, Ghetto Music: The Blueprint*
Digital Underground *Sex Packets*
Doug E. Fresh *Oh My God!*
EPMD *Strictly Business, Business As Usual, Unfinished Business, Business Never Personal*
Eric B & Rakim *Paid In Full, Follow The Leader, Let The Rhythm Hit 'Em, Don't Sweat The Technique*
Ice-T *Power, The Iceberg: Freedom Of Speech . . . Just Watch What You Say, O.G Original Gangster*
Just-Ice *Back To The Old School*
LL Cool J *Radio Bigger And Deffer, Walking Like A Panther, Mama Said Knock You Out, 14 Shots To The Dome*
Mantronix *King Of The Beats Anthology*
Marley Marl *In Control Vol.1*
N.W.A. *Straight Outta Compton, Efil4zaggin*
Public Enemy *Yo! Bum Rush The Show, It Takes A Nation Of Millions To Hold Us Back, Fear Of A Black Planet, Apocalypse 91, Greatest Misses, Muse Sick-N-Hour Mess Age*
Run-DMC *Run-D.M.C, King Of Rock, Raising Hell*
Salt n Pepa *Hot, Cool & Vicious, A Salt With A Deadly Pepa*
Schoolly D *Schoolly D, Saturday Night: The Album*
Slick Rick *The Great Adventures Of Slick Rick*
Stetsasonic *On Fire*
T LA Rock *It's Yours*
Ultramagnetic MCs *Critical Beatdown*
Whodini *Whodini Escape*

Golden Age 45 King *The 900 Number*

Alkaholiks *21 & Over, Coast II Coast*

A Tribe Called Quest *People's Instinctive Travels And The Paths Of Rhythm, The Low End Theory, Midnight Marauders*

AZ *Doe Or Die*

Beatnuts *Intoxicated Demons*

Black Moon *Enta Da Stage*

Black Sheep *A Wolf In Sheep's Clothing*

Black Star *Mos Def & Talib Kweli Are Black Star*

Blahzay Blahzay *Blah Blah Blah*

Busta Rhymes *The Coming, When Disaster Strikes*

Camp Lo *Uptown Saturday Night*

Company Flow *Funcrusher Plus, End To End Burners*

Coup *Genocide And Juice, Steal This Album, Party Music, Pick A Bigger Weapon*

Crooklyn Dodgers *Return Of The Crooklyn Dodgers*

Craig Mack *'Flava In Ya Ear'*

Cru *Da Dirty 30*

Cypress Hill *Cypress Hill, Black Sunday, Temples Of Boom*

DAS EfX *Dead Serious*

DC Basehead *Play With Toys*

De La Soul *3 Feet High And Rising, Buhloone Mindstate, De La Soul Is Dead, Stakes Is High*

Del Tha Funkee Homosapien *I Wish My Brother George Was Here*

Diamond D & the Psychotic Neurotics *Stunts, Blunts And Hip Hop*

Dr Dre *The Chronic, 2001*

Eazy-E *Eazy-Duz-It*

Erick Sermon *Double Or Nothing*

Gang Starr *Step In The Arena, Daily Operation, Hard To Earn, The Ownerz*

Geto Boys *The Geto Boys, We Can't Be Stopped*

Ghostface Killah *Ironman, Supreme Clientele*

Goats *Tricks Of The Shade*

Goodie Mob *Soul Food*

Gravediggaz *Niggamortis*

Group Home *Livin' Proof*

GZA/Genius *Liquid Swords*

Ice Cube *Amerikkka's Most Wanted, Death Certificate, The Predator*

Jeru the Damaja *The Sun Rises In The East, Wrath Of The Math*

Jungle Brothers *Straight Out The Jungle, Done By The Forces Of Nature, Raw Deluxe*

JVC Force *Strong Island*

KMD *Mr Hood, Black Bastards*

Kool G Rap and DJ Polo *Wanted: Dead Or Alive, Road To The Riches, 4, 5, 6*

Kool Keith 'Sex Style', 'Slide We Fly'

Kwest the Madd Ladd *This Is My First Album*

Lord Finesse *Funky Technician, Return Of The Funky Man*

Luscious Jackson *In Search Of Manny*

Main Source *Breakin' Atoms*

Masta Ace *Take A Look Around, SlaughtaHouse*

Method Man *Tical*

Mobb Deep *The Infamous, Hell On Earth*

M.O.P. *Firing Squad*

Movement Ex *Movement Ex*

Nas *Illmatic*

Naughty By Nature *O.P.P.*

New Kingdom *Heavy Load, Paradise Don't Come Cheap*

Notorious B.I.G. *Ready To Die*

O.C. *Word... Life*

Ol' Dirty Bastard *Return To The 36 Chambers: The Dirty Version*

Onyx *Bacdafucup*

Organized Konfusion *Stress: The Extinction Agenda*

Paris *The Devil Made Me Do It, Sleeping With The Enemy, Guerrilla Funk*

Pete Rock *All Souled Out, Mecca And The Soul Brother, The Main Ingredient* (all with CL Smooth), *Soul Survivor*

Pharoahe Monch 'Simon Says'

Pharcyde *Bizarre Ride II The Pharcyde, Labcabincalifornia*
Raekwon *Only Built 4 Cuban Linx...*
Real Live *The Turnaround*
Redman *Whut! Thee Album, Dare Iz A Darkside*
Showbiz & A.G. *Runaway Slave, Goodfellas*
Smif-N-Wessun *Dah Shinin'*
Smoothe Da Hustler *Once Upon A Time In America*
Snoop Doggy Dogg *Doggystyle*
Souls of Mischief *93 'Til Infinity*
Special Ed *Youngest In Charge*
3rd Bass *The Cactus Album, Derelicts Of Dialect*
Various Artists *Soul In The Hole OST, New Jersey Drive
    OST, Friday OST, High School High OST*
Various Artists *Soundbombing, Soundbombing II,
    Lyricists Lounge Vol 1, Definitive Jux Presents,
    Farewell Fondle 'Em, Bring Da Ruckus The Loud Story,
    Muggs Presents The Soul Assassins,*
WC and the Maad Circle *Curb Servin'*
Wrecks-n-Effect *Wrecks-n-Effect*
Wu-Tang Clan *Enter the Wu-Tang (36 Chambers), Wu-Tang
    Forever*

Diaspora   50 Cent *Get Rich Or Die Tryin'*
Diplomats *Diplomatic Immunity*
Cannibal Ox *The Cold Vein*
Clipse *Hell Hath No Fury*
Drake *Take Care*
Eminem *The Slim Shady LP*
Game *The Documentary*
Jay-Z *Reasonable Doubt, The Blueprint, The Black Album*
Juvenile *400 Degreez*
Kendrick Lamar *Good Kid, M.A.A.D City, To Pimp A
    Butterfly*
Kanye West *The College Dropout, Graduation, My
    Beautiful Dark Twisted Fantasy, 808s & Heartbreak,
    Yeezus*
Lil Wayne *Tha Carter III*
Ludacris *Back For The First Time*

Lupe Fiasco *Food & Liquor*
Master P *Ice Cream Man, Ghetto D, MP Da Last Don,*
Missy Elliott *Supa Dupa Fly, Under Construction, Miss E*
Mystikal *Ghetto Fabulous, Unpredictable*
N.E.R.D *In Search Of...*
Outkast *Southernplayalisticadillacmuzik, ATLiens,*
     Stankonia, Speakerboxxx/The Love Below
Roots *Illadelph, Halflife, Things Fall Apart, Phrenology*
Rick Ross *Teflon Don*
T.I. *Trap Music*
Young Jeezy *Let's Get It: Thug Motivation 101*

Index